Praise for Ignite Your Ideas

Wonder, imagination, effort, and choice accelerate creativity. The author's suggestions for all this—and more—will inspire readers to get creating!
~Scott Barry Kaufman, PhD—cognitive scientist, podcaster, and co-author and author of several books including *Wired to Create* and *Transcend*

Ignite Your Ideas *is full of surprising insights into what creativity actually is, and how anyone can decide to be creative. This book is a kid-friendly resource that might just be life-changing for kids who haven't yet found a way to make their own kind of magic. (Note: Parents can learn interesting stuff from this book too!)*
~Dona Matthews, PhD—developmental psychologist, and co-author and author of several books including *Imperfect Parenting*

Ignite your Ideas *is a nurturing book, full of valuable information. Joanne Foster provides a plethora of approaches, calling on people, words, ideas, prompts, and suggestions to help readers become more creative. She promotes creative thinking, problem solving, and cognitive skills for kids—and for adults, too. A wonderful book to help us all delve more proactively into our creative selves.*
~Michael F. Shaughnessy, PhD—professor, author of *Women Scientists Who Changed the World*, and editor of *Journal of Gifted Education and Creativity*

Ignite Your Ideas *is packed with inspiring quotes, insightful guidance, and playful strategies. Joanne Foster's creativity shines through with her use of language, and her many unique suggestions for creative projects, adventures, and explorations. This is a warm-hearted, engaging look at creativity for teens and their families. It will keep curious kids sparkling for days! Highly recommended.*
~Paula Prober, PhD—author of *Your Rainforest Mind* and *Saving Your Rainforest Mind*

I'm very excited about your book because your voice is full of genuine care, pragmatism, and balance, which is rare nowadays.

~Milena Z. Fisher, PhD—co-founder and editor
of *The Creativity Post*

Joanne Foster's book on creativity has a nurturing tone. Her words leave one feeling safe and secure to explore, experiment, dream, and act on hopes. Hers is a warm hand on your shoulder. This is so much more than a book about creativity. Yes, it's practical—with 100 ways to kindle creative flames, ignite passions, and spark brilliance, complete with suggested organization methods to support discovery—but, in the end, it's a gentle guide to life and fulfillment.

~Mark Hess—teacher, and author of several books
including *I Used to Be Gifted*

Ignite Your Ideas *speaks to children in a way that opens possibilities and wonder, inspiring them to look both within and at the world around them. Dr. Foster empowers children to be courageous, self-advocate, be aware of their emotions, and embrace change. Packed with ideas and strategies, this book teaches, encourages, and motivates children to live creative lives, full of growth and adventure.*

~Dan Peters, PhD—psychologist, podcaster,
author of *Make Your Worrier a Warrior* and
co-author of *Boosting Your Child's Natural Creativity*

Joanne Foster inspires, encourages, and suggests surprising pathways to being creative, even if you think you are not. She delivers a toolbox of insight and skills to help children thrive in imaginative and fun ways. Do your children and yourself a huge favor—read it.

~Susan Newman, PhD—author of *Little Things Long Remembered*

A tone of vitality pulsates through her book as Joanne Foster taps into this life source of energy. Anchored in wonder and gratitude, curiosity and resilience, her creativity abounds. Her 100 sure-fire ways to ignite creativity offer ideas for kids and families to initiate vivacity and fresh originality into everyday life.

~Gloria van Donge—author of *The Gifted Kid Book Series*

A highly engaging book addressing the awesomeness and freedom of living life through the lens of creativity. The book presents a scaffolding to guide children to find their own paths. Creativity becomes a profound journey existing within every child. The book provides inspirational quotes from creativity scholars, and poses prompts and direction to ignite wonder. End of chapter summaries help solidify concepts. Highly recommend. It really is such a great book!

~Marianne Kuzujanakis, MD, MPH—
pediatrician, and co-author of *Misdiagnosis*

As an abstract painter, I'm constantly seeking inspiration and different ways to renew my creativity. The ideas in this book are fresh and exciting, and they will inspire kids AND adults. The author encourages readers to find and embrace possibilities and to express themselves creatively. Ignite Your Ideas *is motivating and relevant, and it will spark the imagination of anyone wishing to reap the joyous benefits of living life creatively.*

~Rina Gottesman—award-winning contemporary artist

WOW, WOW, WOW. It is AWESOME!! There are so many things I love about this book! The way the author weaves a wide range of relevant examples into a coherent whole is truly inspiring. Readers of all ages will enjoy the accessible style and text. In her friendly, engaging style, Dr. Foster offers a variety of current and historical examples, thorough explanations, practical strategies, and helpful resources that will appeal to young people and all those who support them.

~Jaime Malic, PhD—teacher and leadership
program coordinator, St. Clement's School, Toronto

Impressively researched but practically focused, Dr. Foster's newest book is a go-to handbook for inspiring and sustaining creativity, written for children, youth and those who support them. This work is filled with motivating quotes and wit, supplemented by additional resources, and best of all, chock-full of workable strategies and idea-starters. No matter what form creativity takes, this book provides great support...Brava!

Colleen Willard-Holt, Ph.D.
Faculty of Education Professor Emerita, Wilfrid Laurier University

Ignite Your Ideas

¡Creativity for Kids!

Joanne Foster, Ed.D.

By the author of the award-winning *Bust Your BUTS*,
now there's *Ignite Your IDEAS*.

It's time to fire up your creativity!

Edited by: Molly A. Isaacs-McLeod, JD, LL.M.
Interior design: The Printed Page
Cover design: Kelly Crimi

Published by
Gifted Unlimited, LLC
12340 U.S. Highway 42, No. 453
Goshen, KY 40026
www.giftedunlimitedllc.com

ISBN: 978-1-953360-29-8

Ignite Your Ideas 🔥

¡Creativity For Kids!

This book is for kids twelve and up. You'll discover thought-provoking and useful information about creativity, including lots of tips to help you become more creative at home, school, and elsewhere—on your own, and with family, and friends.

There's no one set approach for reading this book. You can pick whatever order suits you, or jump to the parts that interest you most and then move around from place to place, or read everything from cover to cover. *You* decide.

Softly lit, smouldering, or scorching creativity…You decide that, too!

Table of Contents

Parents who read this will benefit, too.
Sharing this book will help them to help you!

Moreover…
As they read, adults will discover hundreds of incentives and ideas
for reinforcing and augmenting their own creativity.

Dedication

For Cara, Allie, Jake, Sari, and Cooper, with love.
Let creativity warm your soul and brighten your life—
from flicker, to flame, to inferno.

And to my amazing husband, Garry, who is always encouraging,
and whose love and support are boundless as we discover and
enjoy new and exciting opportunities together.

In Appreciation

Thanks to Molly Isaacs-McLeod at Gifted Unlimited, LLC for
her faith in me, and for her unbridled enthusiasm every time I
brainstorm; to Lisa Liddy at The Printed Page for her expertise
in formatting this book; to Molly Isaacs-McLeod for her editing
prowess; to Kelly Crimi for the lovely and creative cover design;
and to all the creators—past, present, and future—whose ideas,
efforts, and experiences stoke my imagination.

Motivational Words about Finding Creative Pathways

Creativity cuts across gender, cuts across culture, cuts across religions—in every way the capacity to achieve the optimal, best of human potential is there beyond boundaries.

We need to find those kids…, and we need to guide them, we need to love them, and sometimes we need to leave them alone to do their own thing.

~Dr. Barbara Kerr,
Distinguished Professor of Counselling Psychology,
University of Kansas, stated in *Take on Talents*,
National Association for Gifted Children Video Clip

Section One: The Light You Kindle

CHAPTER 1

Why Is Creativity Important for Kids?
(And Adults, Too!)

Creativity is always available if you want or need to use it. You can think it through slowly and deliberately, or you can seize it quickly or spontaneously on the fly.

It's like having a superpower!

Creativity is a choice. YOUR choice. And it's a *smart* choice because it will help you develop qualities and accomplishments that you can feel positive about, and share.

Smart choices have always been keys to success. Century after century, and generation after generation, choices have enabled people of all ages to have hope, and to open gateways to learning, well-being, creativity, and more. Whether by means of ancient hieroglyphics scratched on rough-hewn rock faces, drawings etched on yellowed parchment, or high-tech computer programs shared on multiple online platforms, creativity and hope endure. Individuals *choose* to be creative and to extend their abilities and desires, and this can happen any time or place.

The Essence of Creativity

Is there some magic to being creative?

Yes and no.

Wait—how is that possible?

3

Like with magic, creativity involves a little mystery and a sense of surprise. There's excitement, astonishment, and delight. Creativity is something you feel, and embrace, and express, and stretch, and enjoy. It's a decision that can help you to see fresh possibilities for tackling everyday challenges, and to become happier. Creativity is an outlet for your imagination and curiosity, and for the wonder that lies within your soul.

Here's an example.

As I write this, it's the first week of August. You read that and may think, "Big deal."

Well maybe it is, and maybe it isn't. But now read this (from the book *Tuck Everlasting*, by Natalie Babbit):

> *The first week of August hangs at the very top of summer, the top of the live-long year, like the highest seat of a Ferris wheel when it pauses in its turning. The weeks that come before are only a climb from balmy spring, and those that follow a drop to the chill of autumn, but the first week of August is motionless, and hot. It is curiously silent, too, with blank white dawns and glaring noons, and sunsets smeared with too much color. Often at night there is lightning, but it quivers all alone.*

Sure, August is August, and it comes around EVERY year. However, there are SO many ways to describe it, just as there are countless possibilities for describing any month, or day, or any of the things you see, feel, touch, taste, smell, and experience… You can talk, write, and convey your ideas in different ways—for instance, through words, art, dance, puppetry, music, graphs, and other means. You can be brief or expansive. You can share your notions and your knowledge, or not.

You can be bland. *It's August.*

Or you can be creative, like Babbit (quoted above), or like author Sue Monk Kidd, who wrote, *The month of August had turned into a griddle where the days just lay there and sizzled.*

But here's the thing. Being creative is not just about saying stuff in a fancy or dramatic manner. It's not about trying to impress others, or slapping extra paint on your picture, or adding a few high notes to a song. Being creative is about seeking, finding, and grasping opportunities to be original and to go to the next level in whatever you choose to do. It's about cracking open the door to your imagination, and then poking around in there to find new pathways that you can explore, independently or with others. It's about welcoming ideas as they come to mind—ideas that may slowly simmer or briskly boil, or that may be silly, sudden, suspicious, or scientific.

The sheer joy of creating something that you've worked on (imagined, practised, revised, designed, extended, played with) is invigorating. Plus, pleasure ensues from sharing, gaining confidence, and feeling proud of your accomplishments. All good!

Moreover, there's no limit to what you can do when you unleash the promise of possibility and use your mind, energy, and senses to create something that is *yours*. What's amazing about creativity is that it's boundless.

Limitlessness

> *The cartwheel galaxy was created 440 million years ago.*
> —CNN News, August 3rd, 2022

Imagine that—440 million years! It's hard to fathom. Yet humankind still doesn't fully know how galaxies form, how all the intricacies of the brain work, or why Mother Nature and Father Time act as they do. There's much to learn. Knowledge has no limits. Nor does creativity. We know that creativity need not be restricted by time, age, culture, geography, or gender. Your parents, friends, teachers, community, and the entire world can engage in creativity, whether it's in the form of tiny dribbles or vast outpourings.

Each person's approach toward creativity is uniquely theirs. (We'll look at how creativity develops in the next chapter of this book.) What's important about embracing creativity is that it's an expression of the self. It's part of who you are, and it's a springboard to who you will become tomorrow, and all the tomorrows after that. The more often you make the choice to invite creativity into your life, the more you'll enrich your possibilities for the future—the tomorrows that lie beyond the here and now.

Here's another example of how creativity can be a game changer.

You've seen the moon in its various forms (crescent, half, full, bright, partly covered, and so on), and you may have thought about what it might be like to see it from space, or to walk across its surface one day. Astronaut Frank Borman (Commander of Apollo 8, the first mission that orbited the moon, in December 1968), described the moon like this: *It's a vast, lonely, forbidding expanse of nothing rather like clouds and clouds of pumice stone. And it certainly does not appear to be a very inviting place to live or work.*

Well, that's that.

Or is it?

We can think of the moon (or even Earth), as dull or gloomy or scary—or enticing! It has also been described as haunting, mesmerizing, and mystical. Depending on our vantage point, the moon may appear small or large, colorful or bleak, yellow or orange, smooth or lumpy, or even mysteriously facial-like. Indeed, author Margaret Atwood captures this sort of variability in one sentence. *Reality simply consists of different points of view..*

So, when it comes to everyday occurrences, and how you look at the realities of life, what is *your* point of view? You have the option to change up how you observe, experience, and think. You can get close or stay distanced. You can be explicit and matter-of-fact (like Borman was in the quote above), or mildy or wildly expressive about what you see, whether it's the light of the moon or something else. There are so many options open to you. Your thoughts and viewpoints are a bit like a multitude of firecrackers ready to burst outward into the stratosphere.

A little creativity might impact or improve the way you think about and view things, and how your day or week might unfold, making it more interesting and fun. How can you boost your perspectives and ideas so they're more fulfilling, fresh, thrilling, or enjoyable? There's really no limit to possibilities for imaginative wanderings, or the creation of ideas and concepts. (Sometimes referred to as *ideation*.) If you want to bring ideas to life you have to generate, select, and develop them—which takes time and effort. But seeing an idea go from a tiny glint to a glimmery gleam (or a bland moonscape to a beguiling one) can be motivating and intriguing.

Intrigue

Creativity is often sparked by sights, sounds, conversation, activity…

Look at the photo below. What is this a picture of? Is it something *ordinary* or *extraordinary*?

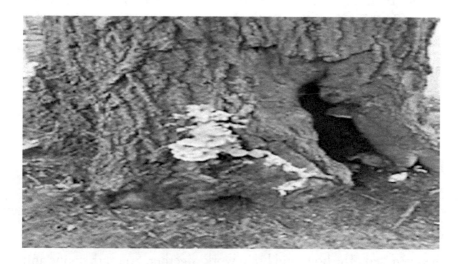

Who took the picture? When? Where? Why? How?

Creativity can also be ignited by questions, and answers. Is that (orange) stuff at the base of the trunk hard or mushy? Is it smelly? Edible? Does it move? What comes to mind when you see it?

Put on a creative lens. Could those be forest pancakes for young animals? Or the roofs of the homes of tree fairies? Or…? Creativity can emerge at a moment's notice, and in relation to any occurrence —making that experience more intriguing!

By the way, that stuff is a fungus. Not a bad thing to encounter but perhaps it's more appealing when you take a creative stance—unless you're particularly interested in examining different kinds of fungi and toadstools, and that can have creative potential, too!

Think in new and unexpected ways. Improvise, dream, explore. Astronaut Borman said, *Exploration is really the essence of the human spirit.* Enjoy explorations, and embrace the freedom and opportunities you have to think, communicate ideas, take action, and create. Reframe your outlook, challenge the status quo, and elevate the ordinary. Be determined. Become aware of creativity around you, through the arts, in nature, within your own neighborhood, in your home. Be innovative. Seek what's unique. Or create it yourself by being flexibly responsive to the things you see and hear. You'll end up bolstering your desires, and learning more as a result!

What's The Relationship Between Intelligence and Creativity?

Intelligence and creativity fuel each other as they develop. When you use your brain, you create neural connections. (Picture millions of squiggly paths inside your head, ablaze with flashes of light.) The more neural connections, the greater your cognitive ability. When you increase your thinking, activities, knowledge, and creativity, you also increase your brain power.

The brain is like a muscle, and like any muscle, it gets stronger when it's exercised. The body and brain work together. Strengthen one and you strengthen the other. When you link your ideas to hands-on activities—such as playing, participating in games, drawing, dancing, writing, and discovering other forms of creative expression—you build your intelligence and grow stronger.

Creative people are good at using what they already know as jumping-off points to learn more. This may have to do with math, or science, or learning a new language, or improving their athletic skills. Their existing knowledge is like a reservoir, and extending their understandings can lead to further discovery, and to adventure, and creativity, too. Here are four tips that such people may be aware of, and now you are, too:

1. Be active and participatory. (That is, show initiative.)

2. Be responsive when opportunities knock.

3. Be resourceful, and get whatever stuff you need in order to advance (such as information, materials, and help).

4. Be willing to push past or to sharpen the edges of what you already know.

Remember, you don't have to change things in grand fashion, like those "creatives" whose work is deemed to be extraordinary, and who may be famous because of it. You don't have to aspire to be creative in the extreme, like highly acclaimed artists, musicians, athletes, writers, or scientists—such as Pablo Picasso, Michelangelo, Andy Warhol, Adele, Beyonce, Elton John, LeBron James, Simone Biles, J. K. Rowling, William Shakespeare, or Albert Einstein. (You can probably think of additional people in these and other domains, too.) Their achievements represent what's sometimes referred to as "Large **C** Creativity." That's incredibly difficult to attain. Not to mention that it takes tons of time, patience, and hard work. Psychologist and creativity researcher Mihaly Csikszentmihalyi defines **"C"** creative people as those whose work is "eminent."

However, "little **c** creativity" is certainly something you *can* aspire toward, experience, and reach. It's reflective of original thought and expression. Csikszentmihalyi refers to "**c**" creativity as more of an everyday occurrence, such as figuring out how to prevent sneaky raccoons or bears from tipping over the garbage can and making a mess. This type of creativity (on the part of people, not wildlife!) also requires an investment of time and effort. It's not "large scale" but it's nevertheless meaningful. It may help you redefine problems or surmount obstacles, reinforce your desire to develop interests or strengths, and empower you to grow into a more creative individual. If you're given the right supports and encouragement from family, friends, and others (we'll talk about that later), *and* if you welcome curiosity and accept opportunities to try something new, then your enthusiasm and your creativity can blossom. Everyone has the potential to be creative. Those who become more creative than others have learned to be so.

LL Cool J had it right when he said, *Stay focused, go after your dreams, and keep moving toward your goals.* He's a hip-hop artist, record producer, rapper, songwriter, actor, and Kennedy Center Honoree, and his words are informed by many years of experience and excellence in multiple creative pursuits. You, too, can shake up the world by using your feet, hands, eyes, mind, optimism…and channeling whatever form of creativity you choose.

But…A Few Concerns

Not everyone appreciates the value of creativity. If the adults in your life don't really embrace creativity in their day-to-day activities, they may not have shown you how it can help you tackle challenges, feel joy, build relationships, or adapt to (and maybe even change) your environment. Therefore, you might not know how much creativity can contribute to pleasure; how music, art, literature, poetry, dance, and other forms of expression can be exciting; and how exercising your imagination with stretches (or maybe lunges) can be fun!

Unfortunately, some parents and teachers don't realize the extent to which creativity can be empowering. (It's not that they aren't well-intentioned. They just may not be fully aware.) However, research shows that children's creativity flourishes when parents and teachers pay attention to kids' interests, talents, questions, suggestions, and ideas.

Ideally, creativity is incorporated into what happens at *your* school, in your *home*, and in the playgrounds, community centers, and other places you visit. If not, speak up—respectfully of course—to let adults know what's on your mind, and what you'd like to try, and why. (This is often referred to as *self-advocacy.*)

It's worth noting, too, that relationships are at the core of creative activities. Friendships and connections enable people to support one another and share ideas. It's okay if you like to be independent and enjoy doing things yourself. But it's good to know that it can be beneficial and pleasurable to collaborate and exchange thoughts with others. Friends and family can offer fresh viewpoints, and be creativity "cheerleaders." Think about how you might connect productively with others. (More on connections in Chapter 3.)

Also, don't be afraid to slow things down sometimes. It can be helpful to just pause, and to find and appreciate the wonder of everyday occurrences, and to pay attention to how they connect with your sense of self. Your feelings (for example, the joy you experience seeing a flower poking bravely through the pavement); your daydreams (the excitement or perhaps questions that arise from unusual ideas that pop into your head); or your sudden flashes of imagination (which can trigger inspirational sparks, such as when you discover something compelling in a museum exhibit or book, or even growing wild on a tree trunk). Take the time to savor these experiences and situations. They can be beautiful beginnings that start the flow of creativity.

It so happens that the word *flow,* specifically as it applies to creativity, has history, including a noted expert's seal of approval. Researcher Csikszentmihalyi coined the term almost 50 years ago while studying happiness. Flow refers to the experience of being so involved with an activity that you become totally immersed, and even lose track of time. Have you ever had this happen to you? It occurs especially when people have clearly defined goals that provide a sense of direction and so they just keep going and going; when there's supportive feedback that lets creators know they're on an exciting track; and when a person feels confident that with enough effort, they can meet the challenges of the task or activity in which they're happily involved, and so become really motivated to continue. Flow can be a way for you to take your enthusiasms to a more focused and higher level. However, be careful not to become so engrossed that you miss other important things—like smoke alarms, important commitments, or family time.

Finally, most kids juggle lots of demands, and the truth is that creativity requires effort and patience. Many kids feel they just don't have enough time to "add" creativity to what they already do. If that's something that concerns you, you're not alone. It might be helpful to get some assistance with skills such as time management, pacing, organizing, goal-setting, and prioritizing. (See *Bust Your BUTS* for tips.) Plus, instead of thinking of creativity as some kind of "add on" try thinking of it as a basic aspect of whatever you do. And, if you're struggling with creativity, check out all the strategies in Chapter 5 here. Since creativity is a choice, you have to *want* to figure out how to make room for it in your activities. This includes making it a point to wind down, relax, play, and reflect during the day, and to let creative ideas flow. It's important to do that!

Going Forward

Anyone can be creative, or crack a door open and ease forward. If you're not an accomplished dancer, can you twirl, whirl, and enjoy moving to music? Sure! If you've never seen a puppet play, can you still become a puppeteer? Yes! If you've never played a musical instrument, can you still become a composer or write song lyrics? Why not? Opportunities are there for the taking. Seek and find! There are music studios, dance venues, conservation centers, online platforms, master classes, mentorship programs, museums, galleries, libraries, and endless resources you can investigate, along with countless activities to try, from sound engineering, to sculpting, to mime—any of which can provide avenues for your creativity.

By way of example (and to show there's always a creative track), eight-year-old Dillon Helbig wrote and illustrated an 81-page graphic novel about time travel and Christmas. He secretly slipped his red notebook onto a shelf in the children's section in a library in Boise, Idaho. He was proud of his story, and he wanted to share it. Within two days, it had been signed out. *The Adventures of Dillon Helbig's Crismis* became so popular that it was entered into the library catalogue, and it now has a ten-year waitlist. Dillon continues to work on storybooks (including one about a jacket-eating closet.). His experiences have motivated other children to write stories, and to seek creative avenues for sharing their ideas, and he has also inspired librarians to offer writing workshops for aspiring young authors. Dillon's desire and initiative have generated creative ripples far beyond his local library.

The best way to develop *your* creativity is to live your life like creativity matters, because it does! Value its benefits, including the joy, increased brain power, the promise of possibility, and more. And pay attention to its development over time. We consider how creativity develops next.

Top Take-Aways from Chapter One

- Creativity is a choice. Each person can decide whether they want to be creative.

- There's joy in creating something. It's invigorating. Share, connect with others, build your confidence, and take pride in your achievements.

- Creativity has no limits.

- Creativity can change your way of looking at and experiencing the world. It can elevate the ordinary, enrich your possibilities for the future, broaden your perspectives, and fortify your ideas so they're more fulfilling, fresh, exciting, and pleasurable.

- Intelligence and creativity fuel each other as they develop. Welcome curiosity, seize opportunities to try something new, and value the benefits of being creative.

CHAPTER 2

How Does Creativity Develop?
Questions and Answers

Since creativity is a choice (your choice), this chapter is about steps you *may choose* to take to help it develop.

Let's begin with an excerpt from a book called *The Dot*, by Peter Reynolds.

> Art class was over, but Vashti sat glued to her chair.
> Her paper was empty.
> Vashti's teacher leaned over the blank paper.
> "Ah! A polar bear in a snowstorm," she said.
> "Very funny," said Vashti. "I just CAN'T draw."
> The teacher smiled.
> "Just make a mark and see where it takes you."

I won't divulge how this story unfolds, or what happens to Vashti. But I can assure you that creativity, like any journey, begins with a single step. One mark, one word, one note, or one stitch can be the beginning of a creative initiative. One step leads to another and another, like stepping-stones on a trail. In time, perhaps your strides may even inspire others.

In the story, Vashti was stuck. She wasn't sure how to proceed, and she didn't have confidence in her ability. Sometimes when I write, I get stuck, too. I look at my blank computer screen and wonder which words (out of millions) I should use. Writing can be difficult.

(It took Peter Reynolds a year and a half to write and illustrate his short storybook *The Dot*.) But writing can be very gratifying, too!

Being creative is like wading into and then rippling still waters, or reeling through space, or travelling among the tangled branches of a tropical forest. It can be scary. The way forward is not guaranteed.

Basically, you have three options.

1. **Stay still.** Do nothing and go nowhere.

2. **Turn back.** And never know what might have been.

3. **Move ahead**. Take a chance.

The third option represents how creativity develops. It involves taking a reasonable risk, a leap of faith.

If you take a chance, it's helpful to have others around who will encourage and support you, providing you with a kind of safety net you as you proceed. Nature writer John Burroughs wrote, *Leap and the net will appear*. Parents, teachers, and friends can help you build your confidence, offer reassurance, and be your safety net. Let go of your doubts, rely on your experience and what you already know. Focus. Have faith in yourself.

That "leap" is one way creativity develops. Here are some more, followed by 15 important questions, and answers.

Fan the Sparks, Create the Magic

My earliest memory of creativity occurred one summer when I was eight years old. A visiting relative brought me a gift of a small box of watercolor paints and a booklet of white paper. I can remember lying on my stomach for hours on our front porch discovering the magic that happened when my wet paintbrush touched the surface of the small hard palettes of paint, and then touched the surface of the paper. The spark in me was ignited!

~Rina Gottesman

Rina is an abstract artist. Decades later she is still captivated by color, line, playful design, and creative energy. She says she tries not to worry about outcomes. She concentrates on the painting process, and on the joy of creating. This can involve mess, chaos, moments of uncertainty, and sudden bursts of inspiration. She sees each empty canvas as an opportunity for self-expression and growth. You may not find many recognizable objects in her works of art, but you will see glorious hues, shading, shapes, textures, and overlays. Rina listens to music or stories while she paints, she evokes what she feels at any given moment, and she will come back to a painting again and again, fine-tuning it over time.

Creativity develops differently for each person. Not everyone is as focused as Rina. Whether you choose to try photography, poetry, or crocheting, or work with stone, clay, or markers, you may find the experience goes smoothly sometimes, and yet encounter challenges and setbacks at various points. Think of these as learning opportunities. Revising, improving, practising, and tinkering is part of the learning experience. Welcome a new perspective. For example, Allie says she does her best thinking while hanging upside down or doing flips, or when she wears costumes, tiaras, or feathered hats. Cara thinks most creatively while she's nibbling on chocolate chips. Sari loves using neon-colored markers to make pictures. Jake gets inspired when he can tie things in with his love of hockey. Cooper is "driven" by trucks. Many kids like to think while in a bubble bath. I often wake up in the middle of the night with zany ideas which I jot down on "sticky notes" so I can revisit them later. Creativity evolves. It doesn't necessarily come forth like a sudden lightning streak.

Get creative while flipping, snacking, drawing, or dreaming of hockey or trucks. Wet or dry. Day or night. It's your call.

What Do Creativity Experts Say about How Creativity Develops?

> *Most experts now see creativity as a dynamic attitude and a valuable human activity, not an innate attribute you're born with.*
>
> ~Dona Matthews

Aha! Creativity is about *doing*, and *thinking*, and *how you apply yourself!* Plus, the more you exercise your creativity, the more creative you'll become. You can keep nudging, or even pushing it further—in different directions, and over time. Creativity won't wear out. In fact, you'll probably discover that your creative energy builds up. For example, enjoyment of fairy tales might lead to artistic costume design or animation drawing. Constructive thinking about park safety can lead to community problem solving initiatives. A love of animals could lead to ways to lend a creative hand to organizations that support guide dogs, horse therapy programs, or endangered species conservation. One creative endeavor can be a key that unlocks doors to other possibilities to ponder and probe.

Ever since she was four years old, artist Carling Lauren Jackson has loved sports (especially soccer) *and* art (especially painting). Over time she was able to find a fulfilling way to nurture and combine the two passions. Now in her early thirties, she's an "athlete artist," and she draws colorful and expressive portraits of individual athletes and teams on and off their playing fields, and before, during, and after matches. Her work is inspired by her interactions with sports figures, and by photos of their lived experiences, and she travels the world meeting athletes and capturing their stories on canvas. Upon being invited to paint murals on site at the semi-finals and finals of the 2022 FIFA Soccer World Cup in Qatar, she posted a quote online that reflects her creative enthusiasm, *Let the beauty you love be what you do.* (Source, Rumi.) She then added, *Because you never know where your deepest passions and talents will take you.* She's right! Creativity is more than drawing or dreaming—it's opportunity! It can empower you to grow and flourish in ways you might never have imagined. As this exceptionally talented artist continues her creative journey, her adventures will be worth following!

Experts in the field of creativity seem to agree that the promise of creativity starts early in life. That said, there are several important factors to consider. Here are some useful insights from five different research sources.

1. **Scott Barry Kaufman and Carolyn Gregoire** wrote the book, *Wired to Create: Unravelling the Mysteries of the Creative Mind.* The authors discuss ten points: imaginative play; passion; daydreaming; solitude; intuition; openness to experience; mindfulness; sensitivity; turning adversity into advantage; and thinking differently. Whoa! That's a LOT to think about. (And it doesn't even touch upon flips, bubbles, or snacks.) Wouldn't it just be easier to turn on a switch like a light bulb, and creativity will shine forth?

    Easier, yes. Likely, no.

    Kaufman and Gregoire write that creativity takes time, thought, effort, and more. Creativity is always evolving, reshaping, and building. By way of example, the authors quote famous artist Pablo Picasso who said this of his own creative process, *A painting is not thought out and settled in advance. While it is being done, it changes as one's thoughts change. And when it's finished, it goes on changing according to the state of mind of whoever is looking at it.*

    If you check out quotes and thoughts revealed by other "creatives" (painters, poets, mimes, jewellery-makers, graphic designers, musicians, and so on), you'll find that a great many of them share this perception of creativity always being in flux; always a process in the making.

    Creativity is not set. *It develops.*

    Kaufman and Gregoire emphasize that the experiences that young people have can be "formative." In other words, what happens early on in life, or what you choose to do then, can influence what will transpire later. Even many years later. The authors say that play, in particular, is formative, and really important. Play can be imaginative, unstructured, exploratory, multi-sensory, collaborative—you name it. Playfulness will help your creativity develop! They write, *Truly, maintaining a spirit of play keeps creativity and vitality alive as we get older.* You're never too old to play, or to learn from it!

2. **Robert Sternberg** is another noted expert in the field of creativity. His research shows that the factors that support creativity will vary across individuals, and across the ages and stages of their development. That means it's good to try different strategies at different times to see what works best for you. For example, one day you might want to go outside and get more in tune with nature; another day you may need to get more sleep or exercise to increase your energy levels. And, because people are at their most creative when doing what they enjoy, you can always follow Sternberg's wise suggestion: *Find what you love to do, and do it!* (That's exactly what athlete artist Carling Jackson is doing.)

    Sternberg has some additional tips for cultivating creativity. For example, he notes the importance of being tolerant of other people's ideas because even if at first they seem unusual or uninteresting, they can turn out to be enlightening. He also advises that it's wise to be resilient, that is, to keep going even if the way forward seems difficult or your ideas start to sputter or stall.

3. Creativity researcher **Daniel Keating** discusses *divergent thinking*—sometimes referred to loosely as "thinking outside the box"—such as looking at ordinary things in different, unusual, or wacky ways, or coming up with a broad range of possible solutions to a problem. Examples of how to do this might include brainstorming, bubble-mapping thoughts (your own and other people's) or playing with ideas. (There's that word *play* again!) You know how a plant can have several shoots, and a game can have many variations, and a river can have lots of tributaries? So, too, can a single idea be a starting point for additional or

divergent ideas. You can think divergently while doing arts and crafts, experimenting with cooking recipes, doing chores around the house, using playground equipment, or participating in other activities. In doing so, you kindle your creativity. Developmental psychologist Dona Matthews (cited above) describes this as *the sparkle of imagination shining through.*

In addition to trying divergent thinking, Keating also suggests paying attention to three more key aspects of creative development:

○ **Strengthen your knowledge and skill sets** so you can build upon them.

○ **Think critically** so you can decide what ideas are worth pursuing.

○ **Communicate your ideas** so you care share your creativity such as songs, poems, woodworking projects, or pictures.

Keating says it's important to balance divergent thinking with these three aspects to maximize productive creativity in different areas, whether it's visual arts, technology, interpretive dance, or other forms of creative expression.

4. What does "success" mean to you? Your notions of success can affect your creativity! The more successful you feel about something, the more likely you are to keep at it. But that doesn't necessarily mean you have to get high grades or compliments. There are other factors that merit some thought.

Creativity expert **Felice Kaufmann** defines success like this: *Knowing what your needs are, and knowing how to get them met without hurting anybody.* She says that success and personal satisfaction don't have to be based on achievements but rather should be predicated on finding ways to make yourself happy. Strategies for this include doing things that are fun; putting an emphasis on process (what you're doing) not product (the outcome); making meaningful connections between your interests and compulsory school activities; and taking pleasure in small accomplishments. It also helps to have (or to think about), various models of success—different people who are living successful lives in different ways—such as artists, computer programmers, athletes, paramedics, pilots, chefs, teachers, and others who are strategic and creative in whatever they do.

Kaufmann also has some proactive suggestions to help kids bolster their creativity:

○ Be innovative by building **remote associations.** Think of how unlikely things connect and then use your imagination to stretch those connections. For example, how do dance moves connect with sleep, or how do train tracks connect with idea formation? Build on possibilities.

○ Become involved with **service projects**. Contribute to the greater good within your neighborhood or the broader community. Forge relationships, help to solve problems, be charitable.

○ Try using *idea traps*. That is, record creative ideas right when they're happening, and then you can release and further develop them later when you have time.

Kaufmann has done extensive research in areas of creativity and learning and, most notably, with U. S. Presidential Scholars, and she offers this solid advice: *You don't have to be "smarter than" or "better than" others. It's okay to be "different from" them.* Creativity is a means for that. Creativity can lead to self-assurance, personal satisfaction, and self-fulfillment, and that can translate into success.

5. Educational consultant **Susan Daniels** and psychologist **Dan Peters** wrote a book for parents titled *Boosting Your Child's Natural Creativity*. The authors share information about creative development, including this (on page 17):

> *Starting in infancy, children are biologically determined to observe, explore, and interact with their environment. Early on, they develop the capacity for imagination and make believe... As children mature, their creative pursuits become*

more structured and purposeful, often with products in mind, and they benefit enormously when given the space and time to create, imagine, and innovate.

If you reread that quote, you'll see some key words, such as *observe, explore, interact, imagination, space, time,* and *innovate*. Each of these is integral to the development of creativity. It makes sense, therefore, to try to be watchful and alert; to investigate the world around you; to connect with others; to be imaginative; to give yourself ample space and time to think, inquire act, and react; and to tap your senses and use your mind to originate ideas—and then seize opportunities to extend them.

How can you do that? Read on…

Find Your Moments of Creative Energy

In the article "Early Morning Musings" in *The Creativity Post*, I wrote this:

When I woke up this morning, I looked out the window and saw the sun rising through branches and sparkling over the lake. The sky was sapphire blue. A deer was nibbling a tree. It was a beautiful way to start the day. It was also a stark reminder that I must take more time to be aware of the wonder of nature. It's both calming and inspiring.

Early morning provides me with a chance to think quietly, and this empowers my mind, body, and spirit. For me, it's like recharging a battery so it can energize my day.

What's a recharging time for you? Morning? Afternoon? Evening? Late at night? Give it some thought. You know yourself best. Honor your whims and preferences. Make the moments that matter to you matter even more. If you get frazzled, be mindful of how you might recapture the calm or vitality or confidence or whatever else you need to carry on.

Personally, I move from one dawn to the next. Sunrises, nature, and new beginnings bring me joy and inspiration. I love the optimism conveyed by poet Maya Angelou's words, *This is a wonderful day. I've never seen this one before.*

In between sunrises, I look for opportunities to use my imagination, strengthen relationships, increase my abilities, be kind, and nurture my creativity. It's a full agenda, and I have many responsibilities, so I don't always succeed in everything. But I try.

However, maybe sitting quietly while gazing at the sky, watching a deer, or appreciating the beauty of the countryside is not your thing for charging up creativity. Perhaps you prefer to walk, run, dance, listen to music, or stretch. (Have you ever heard Raffi Cavoukian's song, *"Shake Your Sillies Out?"* Well, you can do that, too!) Find your own rhythm and way of carving out intervals during the day to spark your creativity. You can do things on your own or with friends. Check out new trails, gardens, books, flavors, melodies, colors—and discover how to make a positive difference in your own life, and the lives of others.

Psychologist P. Susan Jackson writes about the importance of *flexible attunement to who we are, who we are becoming, and where we find ourselves.* She states that *true development is multidimensional and fully rounded,* and that this involves paying attention to what drives you—including emotions, intellect, imagination, spiritual beliefs, and more. She emphasizes that learning and understanding require "processing," which she says is a matter of "becoming aware" of what is happening around you. Life is meant to be experienced, enjoyed, and understood. Changing and developing outlooks—and insights—begin with awareness. Be aware of your surroundings, and be self-aware, too, by thinking about what motivates you, and what enriches your day and creativity.

You probably know that there are many books written for parents and teachers, filled with valuable information about how to help children improve their creativity. But, at the end of the day (or at the beginning of it), it's up to *you*!

A great way to take control is to use your curiosity.

Why Curiosity?

> *"Why do we do that?" leads you to question old assumptions.*
> *"What if?" opens your eyes to new possibilities.*
> *Inquisitive people are catalysts for learning.*
>
> ~Adam Grant

Adam Grant is a writer and a professor, and he asks lots of questions.

So do I. For example, I wonder, do flowers have feelings? Which are more important, numbers or words?

Perhaps you want to know what to do if you encounter a coyote or a fox? Or who invented eyeglasses? Or why iguanas sometimes fall from trees?

You don't know what you don't know until you ask. Should you speak up? Should you be persistent? Should you be curious?

Absolutely!

Albert Einstein was a theoretical physicist, and arguably one of the smartest people in recent history. He said, *I have no special talents. I am only passionately curious.* He believed that curiosity empowered his learning and creative thinking.

Curiosity can fuel intelligence, hopes, and dreams, and help you push beyond what you know or what you can already do.

To that end, here are three questions you can ask yourself:

1. **What do I already know?** Remember, knowledge is the basis for creative thought and expression. It's like a fire-starter, or propellant.

2. **How can I take what I know and apply it?** Effectively? Creatively? Collaboratively? In challenging situations?

3. **What resources are available?** Who can offer advice or support, and provide materials?

Don't be afraid to ask questions, or to request what you need, such as supplies, guidance, feedback, and opportunities to go, and see, and do! For example, are you curious about climate change? Farming? Volcanoes? Sports? Parrots? You can talk with others about your curiosity, your sense of wonder, and how you can acquire information, answers, and opportunities to experience learning—and master challenges that will motivate you and enable you to advance further.

Curiosity can embolden you by getting you into "action mode." That is, away from screens or off the couch so you can interact meaningfully with others. In a series of podcasts, host Stephen Barkley asked me if creativity has to do with "purposeful action." I responded, *Yes!* In fact, that's a great way to think about it. Creativity is not necessarily about coming up with some sort of product (although that might occur), but rather it's about activating your mind and nurturing your ideas. Having a sense of purpose is an added bonus. It's like having your own personal GPS (Global Positioning System) to help direct you as you proceed.

Here's an interesting bit of information. Walt Disney was a famous illustrator, film maker, producer, and entrepreneur. He lived from 1901 to 1966, before the era of GPS systems and computer access, so he did not have benefit of the many kinds of sophisticated and modern-day technological means now used for animation, resource gathering, and collaborative endeavors. Nevertheless, Walt Disney's achievements exemplified "purposeful action" and creative expression. He was involved in over 80 films, received many awards, experimented boldly with innovative methods of animation and live-action production, and made a significant contribution to, and impact on, the film industry. He said, *When you're curious you find lots of interesting things to do.* (And, I daresay, ways to do them!) He recognized that curiosity stimulates questions (who? what? where? when? why? how?), and it leads to answers, and fortifies purpose, too. In fact, did you know that Walt Disney was afraid of mice? He got past that, let his curiosity and creativity surge, and voila—we have Mickey Mouse. Created in 1928, that may have been the start (or dawning) of what has since become a ginormous creative empire!

What might dawn for you? What avenues can you investigate? Magic, mapping, mazes, magnetic forces...? You can acquire resources through multiple access points across a wide spectrum, and follow your passions. Be proactive! Each day is a chance to learn new things—to gather information, respond to it creatively, and then beam it out proudly. In her book *Insight into a Bright Mind*, neuroscientist Nicole Tetreault writes, *There is no better time than now to open up to all your wonder and possibility.*

Interestingly, curiosity is piqued in much the same way that creativity develops—deriving from dialogue, sharing, understanding, and thought. Both curiosity and creativity involve building upon knowledge. Be purposeful. Ask questions, get answers!

Kids' Questions about How Creativity Develops

Here are some questions kids ask, along with some brief answers.

---

1. Emotions—What's the connection between my feelings and my creativity?

The way you feel has a direct impact on what you do or *want* to do. If you're sad or upset, you may not be keen to do anything that requires creative thinking. If you're happy or excited, you might be eager to participate in activities or try something new. Feelings of strength and confidence are emboldening, whereas feelings of doubt can make you shy away from things. Feelings ebb and flow like tidal waves, so what you feel now may differ from what you feel later. Psychologist Eileen Kennedy-Moore has written extensively about feelings, and she says, *When we're not mentally standing back and judging ourselves, we are free to listen, and learn, and try, and experience, and do, and care....* Psychologist and researcher Barbara Kerr is of the same mindset, and notes that, *Feeling free is emotional and motivational.* She says, *Emotions can be thought of as the 'colors' or the 'music' of our motives.*

Pay attention to your feelings, and what might be causing them. Use positive feelings to launch creativity, and reframe negative feelings by thinking constructively instead. For example, let's say a kite you design doesn't fly well. You can still take pride and pleasure in knowing that you tried, you painted it beautifully, and you learned a lot about aerodynamics for next time!

---

2. Senses—How can I use the five senses to increase my creativity?

If you spend time outdoors across the seasons, and at various times of day and night, you'll find many opportunities to see, hear, touch, taste, and smell. Poet E. E. Cummings wrote, *The world is mud-luscious and puddle-wonderful.*

Interact with natural surroundings such as green spaces, parks, conservation areas, beaches, forests, and fields. Go on nature walks and exploratory hikes and outings with friends and family. Take pleasure in seeing wildlife, rushing streams, unusual rock formations, brightly colored flowers, animal tracks in the snow, birds peeking through tree branches, and other sights and sounds. These experiences will enhance your mindfulness (awareness of being in the moment), spark your curiosity, boost your creativity, and help you become more appreciative of nature.

---

3. Parents—How can my parents support my creativity?

Since creativity develops from engagement in different types of learning, your parents can help to ensure you have opportunities to choose what to pursue. They can encourage your involvement in activities, especially ones that match up with your interests and ability levels so that you'll stay motivated. Your parents—and other family members—can cheer you on as you prepare for creative expression, assembling and organizing various materials, or setting aside space you might need. They can reinforce your progress and persistence as you proceed. They can also offer you safe passage to learning and growth at home, elsewhere in your community, and beyond. (More about this in Chapter 4.)

4. Teachers—What can my teachers do to support my creativity?

Don't be afraid to tell your teachers if you want additional opportunities to be able to include creative aspects in your assignments and daily tasks at school. Think about some possibilities, and then sit down and discuss these together.

Teachers can be mindful of your individuality. Creativity can and should be infused into classroom instruction and curriculum content, and with some effort and ingenuity can be aligned with your interests, abilities, extracurricular activities, and what you like to do at home. You know how Superheroes all have individual capabilities? These had to be *nurtured*. It's great to learn math, language skills, science, history, and all the other subjects at school, but if you're not encouraged to develop your unique capabilities then there's a disconnect. You can help your teachers become more attuned to what you're super-interested in, your talents, and your creative impulses (both inside and outside the school walls) so everything can mesh together!

Four more strategies:

- ○ Teachers can help you forge meaningful relationships with classmates so that you can share ideas and enjoy learning together.

- ○ They can provide support and guidance as you advance.

- ○ They can show you how to build skills and knowledge.

- ○ Teachers can motivate you to inquire, make discoveries, and stretch yourself to higher levels of achievement in different subject areas.

In one of her blogs, psychologist Mona Delahooke points to two *life-changing qualities of extraordinary teachers*. Can you guess what they are? (Or perhaps think of ones that are top-of-the-list for you?) According to Delahooke, the first quality is that teachers can *provide a warm, calming presence,* and show you how to stay calm and feel safe. She says that this is *the optimal condition for creativity.* The second quality has to do with building a good relationship with students by *connecting* and *engaging* with them.

You can start by giving your teacher some keys about how you feel, why creativity matters to you, and ideas you'd like to pursue, so that together you can unlock any perceived "closed doors" that might be blocking your flow of creativity at school.

---

5. Expectations—What if the expectations are unfair?

Sometimes parents or extended family can push you to do too much, or they may be too judgmental (as in critical, or nit-picky) about your achievements. Or, you may feel that their praise, pride, and joy are excessive or stifling. If that's the case, speak up. You can help your parents appreciate your concerns, your hopes, and the value you place on your creative expression. Familial support is important, but it's best if it feels reasonable. It's great to try and go to next levels in what you do (that's development in action) but it's most effective when it's fair and suitable, and when motivation comes from excitement not duress.

Expectations at school can also pose a problem if they're not fitting or fair. Speak with your teacher if you feel that's the case. Ideally, every student should be involved in co-creating their goals because that helps to ensure that learning tasks are appropriate, relevant, and motivating. It's hard to be creative when you're unhappy about the way in which goals are set forth, so have a candid conversation with your teacher so you can improve matters together.

---

6. Sharing—What if I don't want to share my creative ideas?

That's okay. Sometimes people don't want to share a work in progress, or they're afraid someone else won't appreciate it, or that they might even steal or distort the ideas. I don't invite people to read my articles until they're finished because I want to refine them first. I often return to them repeatedly, over time and with fresh eyes, and do several revisions before I get to the point of sharing. Eventually I do!

It's worth noting that by communicating ideas and sharing creative products *when you're ready,* you can get valuable feedback, acquire new viewpoints, and enrich someone else's day. Actor Leonard Nimoy (Star Trek's Spock) said, *The miracle is this: the more we share the more we have.* Sharing is a choice. It's yours to decide what, when, where, how, and with whom.

7. Making a Difference—How can I use my creativity to help others?

Creativity offers the potential to problem-solve, and to facilitate positive change. Historian Arnold Toynbee called creative ability *mankind's ultimate capital asset.*

Whether in arts, science, literature, philosophy—indeed any domain—advancement across our planet will be spearheaded by those who think creatively and analytically, and who are willing and able to adapt to changing circumstances. Creativity empowers us to deepen and broaden our thinking, and to find means of tackling difficulties and adjusting to uncertainty. Of course, it's important to learn factual material (at home, school, or elsewhere), but a creative vibe complements knowledge. Creativity brings new perspectives to light, helps people surmount obstacles, and enables them to envision and try unusual ways of doing things. Moreover, leadership possibilities often evolve when creativity melds with connectivity. Idea-extending and idea-sharing can be fun and beneficial. So, pursue your strengths and interests, ask questions, and engage your imagination. Your inspiration and interactions will be personally satisfying, and they can make positive differences in the lives of others, too.

8. Making Money—How can I earn money from my creativity?

Entrepreneurship is a word used to describe the monetization of "stuff" that people invent or develop. (That is, they can make money from it.) Examples might include writing a story that attracts the attention of a book publisher, painting a series of pictures that a gallery owner chooses to sell, or designing kitchen gadgets that simplify cooking processes or baking techniques. Services can also be monetized, such as dog-walking, hair braiding, or lawn and garden maintenance. Creative inventions, products, or services that fill gaps or provide solutions to an existing problem may draw prospective buyers or investors. (Have you ever watched *Shark Tank* on television? People pitch their ideas to a panel of investment moguls, in the hope that their creative endeavors will become highly profitable business ventures. It can be extremely exciting!)

However, it doesn't happen all that often. Countless inventors, authors, artists, and musicians still await their moments of entrepreneurial triumph. So, don't expect sums of money to just come flying your way like leaves on a windy autumn day. There are many considerations, such as product refinement, patents, marketing, production, distribution, sales, and more. The smart thing to do is to be as creative as you can be, keep developing your ideas, and have fun. You can also consult with trusted adults who know the ins and outs of business (especially in the area you're interested in); work with a mentor; or read up on the steps that lead toward entrepreneurial success, including real-life stories of those who have tried and failed to sell their creative ideas and products, and those who have tried and succeeded.

There's a LOT of learning required to become an entrepreneur—at any age. If at some point you're able to make money from your efforts, consider that a bonus. (Not to mention yet another learning experience!)

9. Fun—If it's not fun why should I bother?

Not everything we do in life is jolly or exciting. Creative journeys can be time-consuming, work-laden, and challenging. However, happiness can ensue when we invest effort in something that's interesting and meaningful, even when it's demanding. A creative journey may not start off as fun, but it can lead to pleasure, increased confidence, innovative ways to solve problems, and new connections. A. A. Milne wrote, *The sun still shines even when it's hiding.* See if you can find some element of fun or joy in an activity that might seem to be dull or unappealing.

---

10. Talent—Do I have to be talented at something to be creative?

No, although when domain-specific talent is part of the mix, creative experiences will likely occur at a higher level. Some people just seem to be innately talented in some areas, such as mathematics, singing, dancing, sculpting, or sports. Other people don't have a particular flair or forte. However, if a person works hard, practices deliberately, uses their intellect and imagination, asserts themself and then gets the training they need, they can strengthen their capacities.

Talent development emerges from effort, perseverance, and opportunities to grow, but even when these variables are in place, talent may be elusive. Individual differences in experiences, temperament, ambition, personality, schooling, family dynamics, and supports, all have a bearing on developmental pathways, and there's no guarantee that talent will result. That doesn't mean an individual can't be creative, or enjoy a creative journey. End products may not be as sophisticated or intricate as those created by people who are more talented, but don't let that inhibit you from exploring possibilities and making headway!

Connect your ideas to what you know and to the strengths that you have, and build from there. (See Chapter 5 for more on talent—or possible lack there-of—in relation to creative struggle.)

---

11. Assessment—Can creativity be marked or reliably measured?

There's controversy about this. There are many different tests of creativity, and these are sometimes used to acquire information about how people express themselves, and to what extent they might have original ideas. Creativity testing can involve having to generate a bunch of ideas in certain situations, or work with certain materials, or engage in problem-solving activities—with an emphasis on products, and a focus on usefulness, uniqueness, form, attractiveness, or other factors.

In general though, creativity is too complex to be reliably quantified (that is, assigned a grade or numerical value), and in any case, to what end? Your creativity will be affected by motivation, attitude, perceived challenge, encouragements, desire, and more—most of which can't be quantified either. It's better to understand what propels creativity and to foster that, rather than trying to measure it.

---

12. Opinions—Is a three-headed purple dragon creative or just silly?

Everyone is entitled to their opinions, but you don't necessarily have to agree with them. In fact, differences of opinion can be powerful motivators. Great things have been accomplished by people who have balked at nay-sayers, defied trends, ignored conventional ways of thinking, and opted to stir up controversy. You shouldn't have to defend your creative ideas. Nor do you have to yield to the opinions of others.

There's an old saying, *Beauty is in the eye of the beholder*—so your outcomes could evoke a wide range of responses such as beautiful, wacky, surprising, or colorful. And that's okay! If you want to draw a purple dragon (ostrich, cookie, rock formation, cloud) with or without heads (claws, arms, eyes, warts), then go for it! You can also write about it, compose a song, or improvise a play. However, spending time fussing over what other people might think could be troublesome because you'll short-circuit your enthusiasm, and your creativity.

Opinions do not have to define how you think, feel, or express yourself. Ancient philosopher Plato wrote, *Opinion is the medium between knowledge and ignorance.* Indeed, opinions may lie somewhere in that so-called middle ground—or they may be good or bad, constructive or destructive, relevant or insignificant, carefully pondered or imprecise, and so on. Take opinions into consideration if you believe they're important or have merit, then continue to use your imagination unabashedly as you wish.

13. Impact—What if all my creative efforts go nowhere?

Don't worry about it. If you feel pleasure or pride in the creative process that's a positive experience. You can collaborate, reflect, or experiment wildly with materials, words, or instruments without it having to culminate in some sort of final product. You can enjoy messing with ideas, planting them like seeds, and maybe something will bloom later. (Or maybe not.) But don't fret thinking that creative efforts require validation based on whether they make an impact on others or the world. Your creative journey *is* meaningful. Your own personal gains, including satisfaction and learning, are significant.

Remember, too, that creative efforts may take a long time to come to fruition. They can get weighed down or waylaid by other responsibilities that demand your attention, and you may not fully recognize the potential of your ideas till later—so don't be too quick to diminish their value, discard them, or deem them as going nowhere. Plus, you can always come back to them with fresh eyes, renewed purpose, and additional effort.

14. Surroundings—What if everything around me is deadly dull, boring, and not motivating?

That sounds awful! And you don't have to settle for it!

Dreariness and a lacklustre environment can be (yawn, sigh, zzzz) uninspiring. However, there *is* a flip side to that scenario, and it's that consistency and familiar routines can be reassuring, and provide a measure of comfort for enabling your creative expression. So, it's a bit of a toss-up.

But majorly gloomy and monotonous surroundings, especially across the long haul, can be mind-numbing and problematic.

On the one hand, you might find that a safe place where risks and distractions are at a minimum, offers a suitable milieu for thinking, and for cooking up a creative flurry. On the other hand, you may have to think extra-imaginatively, and take some responsibility for bringing in some color, light, excitement, noise, messiness, or whatever else it takes to offset the tedium, and help you morph from "meh" to motivated. Think about who or what can help you make your surroundings more enticing and stimulating. (Need I say that what's required is some individual or collaborative creativity?)

---

15. Instruction—Can creativity be taught?

Yes—to the extent that this book is full of suggestions for upping the ante on your creativity. Plus, the various people in your life who model their creativity are also in effect teaching you ways to enhance yours. However, the crucial thing is to appreciate the *value* of creativity and the inherent joy of *choosing* to be creative. That's where the real learning and development lie—and it's within you.

Early astronomer Galileo Galilei, wrote, *We cannot teach people anything; we can only help them discover it within themselves.*

Do you agree?

Sure, you can be taught how to play an instrument, how to communicate well with words, how to execute dance steps, or how to draw figures—but taking this information into creative realms demands desire, and a willingness to embrace opportunities to think and let ideas percolate. Aspiration can be encouraged, but not necessarily taught. Parents, grandparents, mentors, teachers, coaches, and instructors can help you find and accelerate your momentum—but in the whole scheme of things, you alone must want to reach out toward the immensity of possibilities that lie both within and beyond your imagination. You are your own best "provocateur" (teacher, cheerleader, agent for change), and the choice to develop your creativity ultimately and forever lies with *you*.

So, cheer yourself on, and don't be shy about giving yourself a pat on the back. Share your positive and creative vibes with others. Enhance your own creative development by reading more about creativity and learning when, where, and how to optimize it.

There are many famous quotes attributed to Benjamin Franklin. One of my favorites is this, *Tell me and I forget. Teach me and I remember. Involve me and I learn.*

With that, I invite you to get more involved in igniting your creativity, and to read the chapters that lie ahead!

Top Take-Aways from Chapter Two

🔥 Creativity develops differently for everyone, but regardless, individual paths are apt to be uncertain. Creative expression can be fortified through focus, reliance on experience and knowledge, and faith in oneself.

🔥 Experts in creativity provide insight. They note that creativity evolves, reshapes, and builds (like melodies in the making, or poetry in progress). Experts also say that people are most creative by doing something they enjoy; by thinking divergently and looking at the ordinary in extraordinary ways; by understanding what leads to their personal success; and by taking the time to explore, imagine, act, interact, and react—and innovate.

🔥 Each person has to find their own approach for carving out opportunities to maximize their creativity, and then resolve to keep that momentum going.

🔥 Curiosity is powerful. It fuels creativity, as well as intelligence, aspirations, and purpose. You can exercise your curiosity through wonder, inquiry, conversations, sharing ideas, seeking to understand, and thinking. (And then thinking some more!)

🔥 Kids have many questions—for example, about emotions, senses, parents, teachers, expectations, fun, talent, opinions, surroundings, and instruction. These are all important considerations, and they can have an impact on how someone's creativity will develop.

CHAPTER 3

Seize the Sizzle—Choice, Challenge, Connections, and Change

Plus Three More Sparks!

The beauty of creativity is that it's applicable to everyone, every area of study, every situation, every age, and every place. Imagine what might evolve with some ingenuity and resourcefulness tossed into the mix of every-day life! (The combining of notes, words, dance steps, gymnastic moves, mosaic tiles, food ingredients, or whatever.) Creative sizzle is truly yours for the making. Israeli Prime Minister Golda Meir said, *Trust yourself. Create the kind of self that you will be happy to live with all your life. Make the most of yourself by fanning the tiny, inner sparks of possibility into flames of achievement.*

Brilliant advice! However, if you're going to create a bonfire, you first have to construct a base from which a spark or two can then catch fire, flicker brightly, and ultimately glow. In this chapter, I share four foundational "logs" for building a steady flame. Log #1 is **choice**. Log #2 is **challenge**. Log #3 is **connections**. Log #4 is **change**. Each of these has an incendiary effect on the process of creating, helping to stoke creativity, and keep it piping hot. Let's look at each of these four combustible elements "log"ically, and see why they matter so much. And afterward, we'll look at three additional impactful factors—the *brain*, the *heart*, and *courage*—and consider why they matter, too.

About Choice

The strongest principle of growth lies in the human choice.
                                                        ~George Eliot

You make choices every day. They may be about what to eat, wear, do, say, read, or whatever—and for various reasons. For example, poet George Eliot *chose* to use that pseudonym (pen name) instead of her real one, Mary Ann Evans, because she felt that women authors were not taken seriously. She lived and wrote in the mid 1800s, and her choice, and voice, still echo over time since here you are reading about them over a hundred and fifty years later.

Choices compel you to deliberate, decide, understand consequences, and develop your identity and independence. Choices are empowering! Therefore, opportunities to ponder, and the ability to choose, should not be taken lightly. These are gifts, and every day provides new gifts. However, the key is whether you *choose* to use them!

When kids are given choice, and take ownership of their activities, they learn that their choices are respected, and they're more inclined to commit to them, invest energy, and see things through.

People function best when they feel secure, and that's especially true when in throes of working through decisions, making choices, pushing boundaries, or trying something new. Don't be afraid to ask for extra support from your family and friends. This may take the form of guidance, reassurance, materials, or having a calm, safe place or comfort zone. Poet Langston Hughes wrote, *An artist must be free to choose what he does, certainly, but must also never be afraid to do what he might choose.*

Of course, you may also choose *not* to do something. For example, you might opt to back off from a potentially risky endeavor, or lose interest in a task, or lack confidence about your abilities or possible outcomes. However, making a choice is often the first step for turning hope into realities. Indeed, we *all* need to nurture hope.

The world continues to change rapidly, and choices are an inevitable part of life. The most successful people adapt, seize opportunities, and learn to make astute choices. A choice may be easy—a simple this or that, with little or no consequences. Or a choice may be more difficult or complex, and require excessive thought and perhaps even a leap of faith.

It can be helpful for you to think along these lines:

- What's the upside?

- What's the downside?

- What have I done before? How did it work out? What have I learned from that?

- Who can help me?

Answers to such questions can inform your decision-making. The choices you make today can have a slight or a significant bearing on how your tomorrows will unfold. All the choices you make add up over time!

Decision-making lies at the core of choice. Sometimes you'll know exactly what you want to do or create; and sometimes you may be unsure and just guess or pretend to know, and hope (and pray) that you're doing the right thing.

Let's say you want to try woodworking. What materials and tools will you need? Where can you get them? What will they cost? Where will you set up shop? What sorts of projects are suitable for beginners? Is woodworking safe? Who can guide you? Choosing to do crafts such as this is great, but the choice to do so should be based on facts and knowledge.

Whenever you're thinking of embarking on something creative, you have the capacity to decide if you want to be risk aversive or adventuresome, whether to move slowly or dive right in, and if it's better to try a conventional or unconventional approach. Woodworking involves safety equipment, knives, hot glue-guns, saws, and other tools that are far more hazardous than paintbrushes, yarn, or clay. Decision-making should involve information-gathering. This can help you understand options, assumptions, and requirements, and whether you can change your mind. Talk to people, read up on it, and find out what you need to know.

Biologist and anthropologist Thomas Henry Huxley advised, *Try to learn something about everything, and everything about something.* The first part of that quote is idealistic—it's far-fetched and impractical to think that you can learn something about *everything,* although perhaps the operative word is *try.* However, the gist of the second part of that quote certainly makes sense. Learn as much as you possibly can (if not *everything*) about what you choose to pursue. Huxley was very bright, and he followed his own advice, spending his life seeking knowledge.

So, as you begin woodworking crafts, you can gather instructions, guidance, materials, and so on. (It's prudent to have a first aid kit handy.) You may find that everything goes smoothly—or you may run into complications such as difficulty knowing what steps or precautions to take, or how to use the tools. You might get slivers, or become frustrated and wonder if you made the right decision when choosing to try woodworking. Again, talk to people about your choice, sharing your concerns, broadening your viewpoint, lessening your risks, and informing your thoughts. Then you can plan intelligently, and chart a sensible course of action, possibly strengthening your resolve, building your own box or structure (or whatever, with elements of *your* choosing)—or moving on to another creative endeavor.

Remember, people are at their most creative when doing what they enjoy. That enjoyment empowers effort, discipline, and perseverance, which in turn fuel creativity. Stay openminded when confronting difficulties or when redefining problems. Find the positives. Think of film director George Lucas, who decided to do just that. *When I was making "Star Wars," I wasn't restrained by any kind of science. I simply said, 'I'm going to create a world that's fun, interesting, makes sense, and seems to have a reality to it.'* Turns out, it was a great decision!

Certainly, through decision-making people learn to become better decision-makers, including how to weigh pros and cons, how to use opportunities to create, fine-tune, and express ideas, and how to make good choices.

You can fortify your destiny and growth by way of strong choices, including *choosing* to be informed and creative—and paying attention to how, when, where, and with whom—and also anticipating that you'll likely encounter some challenges.

About Challenge

> *Every strike brings me closer to the next home run.*
>
> ~Babe Ruth

Some tasks and opportunities may seem challenging. For example, it can be daunting to come up with a creative initiative (in the arts, science, or other domains), prepare whatever is necessary, manoeuvre through all the steps, and see it through to completion. When people confront challenge, they have to decide what to do, or not do, and face the consequences either way. Nevertheless, taking control of a situation is gratifying, and good preparation for other eventualities of life.

Here are a few ideas to help you deal with challenge.

○ **Appreciate your previous efforts, successes, and creative achievements.** Consider how you've worked your way through difficulties before. Compare a current challenge with one that you've already navigated and mastered. How did you manage to prevail? In what ways were you creative? How might that inform or refresh your efforts now?

○ **Find an optimistic perspective.** Is the challenge you're confronting insurmountable? Is it really that big or bad? Is there a bright side? Can others assist you or help to share the load? Try adding some fun and creative energy by thinking imaginatively. In fact, imagine how proud you'll be once you overcome the issues! Winston Churchill wrote, *The positive thinker sees the invisible, feels the intangible, and achieves the impossible.* Yes!

○ **Pace yourself.** Figure out a sensible timeline for completing the task or activity you are contemplating. Take into account the following: 1) the degree of difficulty (because the more complex, the longer the process), 2) how appealing it is (because if it isn't pleasurable, you won't feel motivated), and 3) whether it's relevant (because if it's not meaningful, you'll be inclined to avoid it). Also, let your past experiences guide you in setting a suitable pace.

○ **How do other people tackle challenges?** You can be motivated by the experiences of others. For example, take a moment to think about the journeys of Olympians, Paralympians, and the supporters who encourage their efforts. Many of these individuals have overcome hurdles (both literally, and figuratively), and have had to manage challenging physical, social-emotional, and other concerns while developing their capacities. Their stories are often motivating, sparking new understandings, imagination, and awe. You can learn from their hard work, resilience, energy, support networks, and desire. You can also learn from stories, biographies, and quotes, and from conversations with many others who share accounts about their experiences, including how they've coped with challenge, fostered their creativity, and triumphed.

The best sort of challenge is one you feel you can master. So, when you have strategies (such as the ones above) for dealing with difficulties, you feel more confident, prepared, and relaxed. Those are just some of the precursors and advantages to being resilient. Being flexibly responsive to obstacles while striving to overcome them is a learned skill set that will serve you well throughout the years ahead and in all kinds of challenging situations.

About Connections

I've written elsewhere and often that those who reach out to others and embrace life collectively become enriched through the experience. It's a reality of life, and worth repeating here. At home, at school, in cities, and in towns, we have myriad opportunities to connect in real time. Technologically, we're also able to reach out and communicate with people around the globe. Indeed, technology journalist Clive Thompson describes the Internet as a medium that enables people to collaborate broadly, and that produces *truly hivelike results*. A hive is rather clever imagery. Given the ongoing rapid expansion of technology, millions of people buzzing about online seems utterly fantastical. Yet, technology advances at speeds that we can barely fathom.

We learn by connecting, communicating, socializing, information-gathering, sharing, and being part of networks. This may be virtual or in person, via a big hub or within a smaller milieu, and through involvement in recreational, academic, cultural, urban, spiritual, or other types of collectives. Connections have the potential to be *transformative*; that is, they can affect the way a person's life unfolds.

Here's another bit of imagery to consider. Imagine a sturdy braided lifeline that you can hold on to and that will offer you support when you feel vulnerable or aren't sure how to proceed. Now imagine that the three braided threads are family bonds, friendships, and community ties. Collaborations and open communication channels across family members, friends, and people within your neighborhood can buttress and accelerate your ideas, resource access, learning, and creativity.

A community is a group of thinkers, doers, or collaborators. Your community may be comprised of people you know from different times, places, and stages of life—through real interaction or online connectivity. (But be safety conscious whenever you embark upon virtual outreach!) Each connective experience you have is also an opportunity to forge yet another community, to meet individuals from different walks of life, and to build relationships. Film director

James Cameron said, *I feed on other people's creativity: photographers, artists of every kind.* That simulating collaborative spirit shines through in his movies (the most recent being *Avatar: The Way of Water*), with powerful stories, colorful visuals, and captivating characters.

How and where can you maximize connectivity? Check out local flyers, community newsletters, neighborhood bulletin boards, and school-based recommendations for extra-curricular options. Consider looking into youth groups, team sports, and mentorships; programs at libraries, houses of worship, and recreational centers; artistic pursuits, including galleries, art shows, museum exhibits, and theaters; and areas of personal or family interest such as social justice, environmental concerns, volunteerism, culture, or science. For example, there are lots of "ologies" or forms of knowledge from A (astrology), through E (ecology), to G (geology), and P (paleontology), to Z (zoology). Perhaps you can join clubs relating to such topics, or clubs where you can engage with people interested in books, chess, craftsmanship, or artificial intelligence. Any of these community-based avenues can help you realize intellectual, social, or other kinds of fulfilment, and fire up your creative and analytical thinking skills, too.

Psychologist and researcher Scott Barry Kaufman notes that people have inner strengths and creativity that they often don't tap into because they tend to focus too much on a *very narrow slice* of who they are—their interests, close friends, and regular daily activities. However, extending outward can be extremely gratifying and help you grow. Sometimes what's needed are other perspectives, encouragement, fresh experiences, or just some human connection. By way of example, in the book *The House at Pooh Corner* (Chapter 6), author A. A. Milne, writes, *You find sometimes that a Thing which seemed very "Thingish" inside you is quite different when it gets out into the open and has other people looking at it.* There can be insight and excitement borne of different points of view. Milne packed a whopping amount of wisdom and common sense into his simple stories with endearing animal characters. His books are in many ways classics for children—and for adults, too—because they illustrate life lessons that are timeless. So, for instance, when Pooh comes up with a game that doesn't work well until he shares it with others, we appreciate that "things" (games, ideas, dreams, whatever), take shape and ignite through collaboration. This is as true now as ever.

Indeed, we've all struggled with a lengthy global pandemic, and our individual and collective well-being has been threatened repeatedly. Families have endured physical distancing, programming interruptions, event cancellations, health scares, and feelings of vulnerability, but we've coped, maintained connectivity, and prevailed.

We're stronger together! Young, old, or in-between, we're bound together by our common humanity. We co-exist here on Earth, and we're co-reliant. We're better when we boost each other up, offer assistance, and respect one another's views. We must value important attributes such as compromise, resilience, trust, empathy, and patience. We can build bridges, and share direction, suggestions, and strategies for overcoming struggles or resolving conflicts. We can try to contribute to society. We can learn what propels other people's creativity, interests, and personal growth, and we can apply those lessons through connectivity channels as we embark upon our own developmental paths, or encounter change.

About Change

> *Change is the law of life.*
> ~John F. Kennedy

Each generation lives through change, and we all sometimes experience uncertainty. Changes may have to do with family circumstances, program transitions, health and wellness, unforeseen events, or other happenings at home, school, or elsewhere.

How do *you* respond to change?

One way is to embrace purpose.

A sense of purpose is like a flame or flashlight that illuminates the way forward—imagine having your own radiant North Star. People who are purposeful tend to know where they're headed. They're focused, and they're more likely to get where they're going and get things done. By combining inspiration and effort in a purposeful manner, they can prepare to confront change.

When change occurs, you have the option to back off, or to strengthen your resolve, and advance. You may need advice, or help, or resources—but at the end of the day (any day) you have to invest in yourself. Be purposeful when change disrupts your status quo.

Much of the change in our world is driven by technology. It's important to become tech-savvy, and to learn how to navigate computer landscapes effectively and, of course, securely. Ongoing and meaningful technological engagement by kids like you (and your parents and teachers) will increase understandings of outreach, respectful dialogue, online safety, AI, and openness to ever-expanding tech-connectivity.

For example, there's a great deal you can learn about the possibilities of educational technology. "Ed tech" combines digital learning tools (such as new programs and apps), and educational practices (such as established strategies for effective learning) that can help you increase your level of technological literacy, and individualize your learning, resource access, and creative endeavors. However, it's important to monitor your online habits by being informed about how to be a smart tech-user. (At the end of this book I've included resources by Devorah Heitner, Joanne Orlando, and Shimi Kang. They each write books and articles on how families can develop healthy online practices.)

As you adapt to change, whether technological or otherwise, it's also important to hold on to and safeguard what matters to you, including your own enthusiasms, curiosity, and ways of being creative. Find time to pursue your interests, and to develop your talents and skillsets. Challenge your intellect. Get involved in extra-curricular activities (arts, STEM [science, technology, engineering, mathematics], literature, athletics, authentic problem-solving, robotics, leadership, etc.). Change them up if you like, but try to make worthwhile choices. U.S. National Youth Poet Laureate Amanda Gorman, who describes herself as *a wordsmith and a change-maker,* wrote, *Change is made of choices, and choices are made of character.*

Sometimes change is upsetting. However, if you believe that you can confront it, and that you can recover from the difficulties you may encounter, you'll gain self-assurance. Stepping out of your comfort zone once or twice gives you incentive to be able to do it again, and again, and again. Amanda Gorman also wrote this poem:

> *I can hear change humming in its loudest, proudest song.*
> *I don't fear change coming, and so I sing along.*

A confident attitude and concerted effort can help carry you through. You can also learn from changes that you've navigated before. Determination is at your disposal, and it need not be used sparingly. Cultivate and use your strengths and adaptability! Author George Bernard Shaw had good insight when he wrote, *Progress is impossible without change, and those who cannot change their minds cannot change anything.* Accepting or adapting to change has a lot to do with perspective—how we look in retrospect (past), currently (present), and foreseeably (future).

We can't predict what lies ahead, including what changes might occur. Nonetheless, it's helpful to try to anticipate change, and to figure out how to use it to advantage. Change can be exhilarating or daunting. It can accelerate or short-circuit your learning. It can also extinguish your creativity—but don't let that happen to you! Focus instead on the possible delight and headway. That is, on the positive aspects, not on the potentially negative ones.

In my favorite movie, *The Wizard of Oz* (based on the story *The Wonderful Wizard of Oz,* by L. Frank Baum), a young girl named Dorothy Gale gets caught up in the eye of a twister. She's whisked away from Kansas to the fictional Land of Oz. Over the course of time, she makes three new friends. Each craves a change. They desire something essential. The Scarecrow wants a brain, the Tinman yearns for a heart, and the Cowardly Lion longs for courage. After a series of adventures (and misadventures involving a wicked witch, a wizard, and other characters), the friends discover that each already embodies the attribute they desire. They just never used it to advantage until they were compelled to do so when ever-changing conditions helped them to appreciate their truth. (More about this story coming up shortly!)

Like these three fictional characters, individuals have the power to develop their intelligence, understand and regulate their emotions, and galvanize bravery. However, changing circumstances, influences, and other factors can interfere with fully activating this triad of personal strengths.

When kids experience roadblocks (such as changes) on their developmental pathways, supportive measures and guidance can lead to solutions. Plus, every child can be encouraged to pay careful attention to the power of their brain, the feelings within their heart, and the strengthening possibilities of courage!

The Brain, the Heart, and Courage

L. Frank Baum's storybook character, Dorothy, develops a creative mindset and an unwavering spirit as she sets about solving escalating problems. She doesn't tire, or get discouraged, or give up. She's supportive of others, and she keeps calm. She makes *choices*, overcomes *challenge*, makes meaningful *connections*, and experiences *change* (all topics I've just discussed). But wait, there's more!

The Power of the Brain

> *At its peak the brain has 100 billion neurons, and can process 1000 signals per second per neuron, with a total brain capacity of 100 trillion basic operations per second. Mind boggling!*
> ~Dona Matthews and Joanne Foster

Dorothy may not have understood brain development, but she did appreciate the power of thinking. She would likely be fascinated to know that brain development occurs non-stop, as the brain creates new pathways, patterns, and networks over time. In 2021 (long after

Baum's story was penned in 1900, and the movie was released in 1939), Neuroscientist Nicole Tetreault wrote, *The brain is a dynamic organ and has the ability to grow based on experience, environment, and genetics.* This is an excellent way to think about *neuroplasticity*—that is, the brain's flexibility, and how it underlies learning.

The more scientists learn about brain development and neuroplasticity, the more we realize that we cannot predict or set limits on anyone's potential for learning. Whether you're travelling along a yellow brick road (like Dorothy), confronting a challenging task, or doing whatever you aspire to do, the brain's awesome capacity for change and growth propels forward momentum.

How can you enhance your brain power?

Brain-building activities can augment many aspects of learning, including your thinking skills, creativity, communication, motor development, and more. No two brains are alike, and no two bodies are either, yet the brain and body work in harmony. It's like having a finely tuned instrument that only you can play. Have a look at the following ideas:

- ○ Puzzles, games, and hands-on explorations are examples of tasks that promote active intellectual and creative engagement.

- ○ Participate in imaginative play and multisensory experiences.

- ○ Make connections between what you already know and what you want to know.

- ○ Collaborate and "brainstorm" ideas.

- ○ Read—and reflect upon what you read. Then keep reading!

The brain can be exercised by many means such as researching, planning, prioritizing, painting, debating, writing, questioning, and pursuing interests—all of which will fortify your brain's neural efficiency, and its ability to stretch.

The Power of the Heart (Emotions)

*The best and most beautiful things in the world cannot be seen
or even touched—they must be felt with the heart.*
                                                    ~Helen Keller

Some feelings are difficult to manage. Disappointment, shame, anger, loneliness, fear, confusion, uncertainty—these are examples of emotions that can tug at the heart, and how you might feel sometimes as you experience your world. Emotions can interfere with your ability to go about everyday activities, and affect your confidence, productivity, well-being, and engagement in learning. Conversely, feelings of joy, optimism, excitement, and self-assurance can be uplifting.

How can you enhance the power of your heart?

Here are some suggestions:

○ Name and accept your feelings. That will help you validate them.

○ Be positive.

○ Try to remain calm. (For basic tips for children, see *When I Am Calm* by Amy Feldman.)

○ Honor your achievements.

○ Listen, observe, be patient, and stay level-headed.

○ Pay attention to how others monitor and regulate their emotions.

○ Ask for professional help if you're stressed or if you're having a hard time managing your feelings.

Connections and support, as well as reflection and self-awareness, can help you deal with issues that might be troubling you.

The Power of Courage

All you need is confidence in yourself.

~L. Frank Baum

There are many synonyms for "courage"—including bravery, daring, nerve, tenacity, mettle, and my personal favorites, pluck and moxie. Courage can help you overcome obstacles or worries, achieve goals, and find new ways forward. Courage may demand confidence, creativity, resourcefulness, and purpose—all of which generate action. You don't want to be reckless, but if you have dogged determination and a sense of adventure, you'll find that you can better follow your dreams, and pursue curiosity and wonder. This, in turn, will lead to greater knowledge, creativity, pride, enthusiasm, and pleasure. In the "olden days" this passion was sometimes referred to as "fire in the belly." (I like to think that it aligns with sizzle in the soul.) Infernos often begin with embers—tiny sparks that grow.

How can you enhance your courage?

When you push yourself to next levels in any area, there's a blending of development and courage. It's also beneficial if you receive praise, reassurance, and reinforcement. These are confidence boosters that can help you acquire more faith in your ability to succeed. *Discover* and *proactively* use your own personal keys to success—keys such as adaptability, patience, your particular areas of strength, a sense of humor, or whatever gives you an edge. Tips for courageously "next-leveling" in creative, intellectual, motivational, or other domains include the following:

○ Persevere.

○ Find relevance.

○ Ask for help when you need it.

○ Maintain life balance.
  (Rest, play, exercise, and participate in diverse family activities.)

○ Visualize success.

○ Reframe negative situations. (See these as opportunities instead.)

○ Take sensible risks.

○ Take creative steps—and strides.

Build upon your courageous moments one at a time as you broaden your experiences, overcome challenges, and fuel understandings. Strive to be the best you can be!

Last Words—from The Wizard of Oz

What would you do with a brain if you had one?

~Dorothy Gale

A heart is not judged by how much you love, but by how much you are loved by others.

~The Wizard

True courage is in facing danger when you are afraid.

~L. Frank Baum

The brain, the heart, and courage—a triple whammy, and thankfully one that *everyone* has the power to value and strengthen, regardless of age. No wizardry required!

However, there IS magic in family life. There's a core message that resonates throughout Dorothy's journey in Oz, culminating with these words: *There's no place like home.* That's the essence of the next chapter.

Top Take-Aways from Chapter Three

● *Choice* is an important aspect of life. Choice requires you to think, make decisions, realize consequences and, ultimately, develop independence. Your choices will have an impact on how (or if) you might turn your dreams into realities, forge and then extend new pathways, and see things through. Life is made up of many choices. Choose wisely, and choose to be creative!

● *Challenges* reflect the many twists and turns of life. Tips for dealing with challenge include revisiting your previous experiences (such efforts, successes, and creative achievements); being optimistic; pacing yourself; and considering how other people tackle challenging situations. All of this can help you become more resilient.

● *Connections*, within the community or beyond, have the potential to broaden your networks, which in turn help you build relationships, enrich your understandings, and inspire ideas and creativity.

● *Change* is inevitable. If you believe in yourself, and your ability to confront change when it happens, you can rise above difficulties, and gain confidence. Try to be adaptable, be willing to step out of your comfort zone, and welcome change experiences as opportunities to gain knowledge and become more creative.

● The brain is a remarkable organ. You can strengthen your brainpower (and creativity and learning) with pursuits such as reading, questioning, following your interests, and finding ways to extend your reach.

◈ Heartfelt emotions can leave you feeling high or low. There are various ways to accept, validate and gain control of your emotions, such as building connectivity, finding the support you might need, and increasing your self-awareness.

◈ Courage boosts determination and aspirations. A brave and adventurous spirit, fueled by curiosity and wonder, can be motivating, and lead to greater knowledge, pride, joy, and creativity.

Section Two:
The Glow You Nurture

CHAPTER 4
Creativity and Everyday Family Life
(It's Not Just Arts and Crafts)

You don't choose your family.
They are G-d's gift to you, as you are to them.

~Desmond Tutu

In the previous chapter I discussed elements leading to creative sizzle—including choice, connections, challenges, and change—and next we'll have a look at how families can nurture and support those elements.

Your family may be big or small; include infants and/or seniors; celebrate events quietly or with gusto; have branches that extend around the world or remain close by; or be a constant or occasional source of amusement, frustration, embarrassment, or joy. Families come in all sorts of forms and combinations. Like hiking trails, clouds, lightning strikes, snowflakes, or fingerprints, they're all different! And they do different things.

For example, one or more members of a family might like doing various kinds of arts and crafts projects—and for many children that's a frequent pleasure and pastime. But there's also Wordle, working on puzzles, camping, biking, or growing fruit and making homemade tomato sauce or strawberry jam. There are SO many things you can do, independently or by bonding together with family. You can engage in a range of activities, support one another's interests, and help to strengthen creative expression. You can read or share stories, create new games, plant a herb garden, try weird science experiments, build forts, invent creative approaches for completing household chores, and pursue interests that may have been put off but are ripe to investigate now. You can co-create a *curiosity-driven* and *exploratory* family dynamic. The possibilities are endless! Plus, families are an optimal hub for strengthening values and everyday "life lessons" such as kindness, reliability, respect, forgiveness, honesty, patience, gratitude, and compassion—and how to contribute creatively to the community.

In fact, there are lots of benefits that accrue from drawing upon the strength of family. Availability enables you to chat. You can comfort one another in difficult times; develop coping skills when experiencing disappointment, frustration, or worry; and offer hugs and humor as needed. Family members can help you filter information and misinformation. They can offer reassurance as you understand and come to grips with your feelings, and encourage you to discover resources so you can answer thorny or delicate questions—together. A family that's fueled by collective optimism, bonding, play, commitment, and love is stronger for it.

To that end, in these next few pages, we'll explore two questions:

1. **How can your family nurture and support your creativity?**

2. **How can *you* help your family nurture and support your creativity?** (In other words, what can *you* do or share to enable them to enable you to be as creative as possible? Does that sound confusing? It's not really. It boils down to you knowing a few basic points about what you and they can try to encourage.)

The suggestions that follow are tried-and-true, and they're grounded in evidence-based research, and common sense.

Here we go.

Question #1—How Can Your Family Nurture and Support Your Creativity?

Firstly, let's take a moment to focus on the words "nurture" and "support." That way we're on the same wavelength.

To *nurture* someone or something is to cultivate or raise it so that it grows. For example, think about an orchid. Before there's even a hint of a flower, a root lies beneath the soil. It can take a long time before one or maybe two stalks finally shoot upward. The root requires nourishment from air, water, and sunlight. If the plant is nurtured in that way, and the foundation (soil) is healthy enough, the orchid will thrive. Tiny buds will start to sprout, and then beautiful flowers will appear. However, there's no guarantee as to the nature of what will bloom, or when. Patience is required.

When it comes to nurturing, kids require more than air, water, and sunlight to flourish. But you, too, can blossom if you have caring supports at home, school, and within your community.

To *support* someone or something is to provide sustenance or help. In the case of children, that would involve encouragement, day-to-day care, and attention to individual needs and well-being, including their safety, and physical and mental health. Supportive measures can make all the difference in how a child will develop—for example, what interests they'll pursue, which values or skills they'll learn, what challenges they'll embrace, and what choices they'll make.

Nurturing and supporting are both essential, and they're also intertwined. They can be difficult to pull apart from one another—but why would anyone want to?

So, let's go back to the question in the heading above, and consider how your family can nurture *and* support your creativity.

Here are three practical ways:

- ○ **Promote life balance**

- ○ **Appreciate individual differences**

- ○ **Be proactive (take initiative)**

We'll consider them one at a time.

Your Family Can Promote Life Balance

What is life balance? It's like having a "secret sauce" that's your very own special elixir, and that gives you the ability to advance. Imagine life balance as a power-inducing way to help you feel in control when you're caught somewhere between order and chaos; too much and too little; light and darkness; or solitude and community. Another way to think of it is as a middle ground between extending yourself too vigorously or too gingerly; between overexerting or being too relaxed. Life balance is about finding and maintaining your *equilibrium*; that is, the stability or steadiness you need to cope with what comes along on a daily basis.

If you think about how you structure your days, there's probably a routine or several activities that are part of the norm. For example, you might start with a morning stretch, brush your teeth, get dressed, eat breakfast, and then head off to school or get together with friends… And, as the day progresses you might have intervals for recreation, reading, snacks, family visits, sports, music, and so on—till evening when perhaps you do homework, relax, get ready for bed, and go to sleep. Each day is comprised of many and varied activities. No two 24 hours are identical though, any more than your day and anyone else's are the same.

However, it's important to try to have a harmonious balance between busyness and downtime. You know how meals over the course of the day should have a "healthy mix" of fruits, vegetables, grains, protein, and dairy? So, too, should the day consist of a "healthy mix" of leisure, schoolwork, exercise, and whatever else makes you feel content and will contribute to your well-being. It also makes good sense to pay attention to your daily (and sometimes fluctuating) sleep require-ments, nutrition, feelings, and various aspects of wellness—and to keep these things in check. This may mean more or possibly less time spent playing, multi-tasking, hanging out with others, being reflec-tive, or igniting your imagination. Every individual, and every day is unique, but *balance* (that "healthy mix") matters. It can make the difference between feeling overwhelmed, underwhelmed, or happily productive. Because, if you feel as though your day is not topsy-turvy or burdensome—if you sense that there is balance and value—you'll be better able to pursue your interests, confront challenges, use your strengths, and find opportunities for creativity. Indeed, family members can encourage one another to set reasonable expectations, and to take shared responsibility for what has to be done around the house or as part of planning for family activities.

Your family might also want to review how engagement with technology factors into things. Do you all have healthy tech habits? Are you *screensmart*? This includes knowing how to find and use safe and quality apps, platforms, and digital frameworks; being careful about online relationships; and learning to navigate virtual venues with confidence and caution. If each person in your family thinks about their computer habits and screen management tendencies, and shares individual suggestions and concerns, this could help to ensure that everyone is well supported in developing positive connections and good digital practices. As the number and types of online portals and digital devices grow, it's increasingly important that family awareness about how to use them keeps pace. Moderation is a big part of it, because although technology has many benefits for learning and creative output, devoting too much time and energy to life online can compromise life balance offline, in the real world. Your family can work together on ideas for balancing computer-based opportunities and challenges alongside other dimensions of daily life.

In truth, the reality of life balance is different for everyone. For me, well-balanced days include interludes of laughter, family interaction, comfort, accomplishment, creative expression, leisure, exercise, connectivity with friends, some computer time, resourcefulness, calm, and playfulness. A balance to be sure, but worth aspiring toward. What factors into your balance? And how can you achieve it? Ask yourself—what's your secret sauce for equilibrium, contentment, and self-confidence from one day to the next? Something to ponder, and perhaps chat about with your family members.

Your Family Can Appreciate Individual Differences

Everyone learns differently, and everyone's creative expression differs, too. Your secret sauce doesn't have to be *secret*. If your parents and family are attuned to how you learn, what you like to do, when you're content (or not), and when you're at your most productive (or not), that's a good start.

You can talk about these things if you want, so your family can better understand what makes you one of-a-kind—why you are your own person, what stimulates your learning, and how you like to express yourself. For example, in the world of flowering plants (like the orchids I referred to earlier), one plant may bend, or take time to bloom, or produce multiple blossoms, whereas another may stand straight, grow quickly, and boast only one or two flowers. Every plant, tree, animal, rock, seashell—and individual—is different. That reflects *diversity*.

Across the globe there's *diversity* of thought, language, culture, architecture, religious beliefs, style preferences—you name it. Poet Maya Angelou said, *In diversity there is beauty and there is strength*. And U. S. President George H. W. Bush compared diversity to stars, *like a thousand points of light in a broad and peaceful sky*.

Your ideas, creativity, and ways of learning exist within the broader sphere of diversity. Some kids function slowly and methodically. Others like to do things quickly, or independently. Still others prefer hands-on involvement, or with an emphasis on listening or observing. No one approach is right. Moreover, they can be combined.

Some kids have trouble with learning and creativity (see Chapter 5). They may be reluctant, or overwhelmed, or distracted, or lazy. There are children who are gifted learners, and who enjoy opportunities to work with advanced or sophisticated academic content, and to engage in higher-order thinking activities (such as predicting, drawing conclusions, and integrating and evaluating concepts), but who become bored and disenchanted when they're not challenged enough. Other kids are disorganized, or confused, or afraid to make mistakes. Or none or all the above!

No matter what kind of learner you are, it's helpful if those around you (parents, family members, teachers, friends) recognize and appreciate your individuality, and respect and support you along the way. Chat with them about the importance of that, and keep the conversation going as you continue to find new things to explore, learn, and create. On page 21 in *ABCs of Raising Smarter Kids* I wrote, *A strong family circle is comprised of people who convey appreciation for one another, stay connected, and are respectful of variations in interests, personal attributes, and capabilities.* In the fabric of life—*your* fabric—let your family interactions be a silver lining.

Your Family Can Be Proactive (Take Initiative)

Here are some practical ways that your family can help you become more creative. The thing is, if you don't tell them, they may not know, so it might be useful to go over these points with them and see how they react, and what they're willing to do.

- ○ **Take joy in each other's accomplishments.** Talk about them, build upon them, share them, and be willing to take next steps together.

- ○ **Read this book together.** Encourage your parents, grand-parents, siblings, and extended family to have a look at the information and ideas throughout this book. They can do this with you, or independently. You can talk about the parts that you (or they) feel are most helpful or note-worthy, or that arouse your curiosity or enthusiasm. What possibilities would you like to take further? Check into some of the resources, and try some of the suggestions.

- ○ **Practice gratitude.** There's a lot that can go right (and sometimes wrong, too) but research evidence shows it's ben-eficial to take stock of what's good in life, and to be grateful for that. *Grateful people are more contented than others. They sleep better. They're healthier, more popular, more resilient, more optimistic, more energetic, and more successful in every realm. They live longer and report a higher level of happiness.*

Developmental psychologist Dona Matthews wrote those words in a December 2022 blog. She suggests starting a family gratitude journal where everyone records experiences, people, or things for which they feel thankful.

○ **Share your hopes.** For me, hope is about visualizing positive outcomes, and sometimes this means I may have to dig deep to find inner strengths. However, when I share my hopes and creative ideas across a broader but trusted spectrum (with family or close friends) I receive encouragement, and thus greater opportunity for growth and pleasure—and potentially unanticipated possibilities, too. Hope is like a beacon, shining forth. Clinical psychologist Matt Zakreski said this in a recent interview, *Hope can guide our actions toward a better future… We can start this process by paying attention to all the good things we are already doing, and give ourselves credit for those good things.* Family can be terrific boosters in that regard!

○ **Communicate openly with one another.** Don't clam up otherwise nobody will know what you're thinking, planning, or desiring—or how to assist you.

○ **Read together.** Share stories, read aloud, find excitement in the pages of books, and let your imaginations run rampant. Pediatrician Marianne Kuzujanakis extols the importance of reading with these words, *Through our imaginations, we are transported to other worlds… We become more than simple spectators, and more aligned and emotionally invested with the actual struggles, hopes, and outcome of the story arc.* Reading provides excellent opportunities for families to discuss their feelings, enjoy books, and build upon ideas.

○ **Seek and find.** Look for experiences such as drama, poetry, crafts, inventing, scrapbooking, drawing—whatever moves you, and at a pace that suits you. Author Eric Carle wrote the classic children's story *The Very Hungry Caterpillar*, and he offered this bit of counsel: *Simplify, slow down, be kind. And* *don't forget to have art in your life—music, painting, theatre, dance, and sunsets.* Great advice!

Question #2—How can you help your family nurture and support your creativity?

Given that we're talking about YOUR creativity, what do you need to know about how parents and family members can encourage you? Being aware of some basic strategies can empower you to help them help you! Creativity can be affected by influences (such as people, places, behaviors, or things), and ideas can come out of nowhere. Small kernels, big pops, or huge explosions! However, you can ignite any of that by interacting proactively and meaningfully with the people you love and trust.

The more you welcome the input and support of your family—those who really know your ways of being, and who believe in you—the greater the chance that you'll discover enticing gateways and worthwhile experiences. Families that create together, grow stronger together!

Therefore, use your voice. You don't have to be loud or flashy. Bring your know-how, ideas, spirit of adventure, qualms, and viewpoints to the family table. Tie them constructively, creatively, patiently, and thoughtfully to the contributions, efforts, leanings, feelings, and learning of your family members—and then develop (and continue to refine) a shared ethic and approach moving forward. Listen, observe, inquire, hug, be flexible, and slow down if need be (as Eric Carle suggested) because days can be unpredictable whirlwinds of activity.

Be considerate. Remember that a simple smile, nod, thumbs-up, or pat on the back can be delightfully encouraging. People's happiness and well-being depend upon what author Stephen Pfeiffer refers to as *heart strengths*. These include respect for others, compassion, humility, integrity, and forgiveness. Families can learn and demonstrate these important strengths, and as part of a family unit, *you* can help to model and enforce these attributes.

What else can you and your family pay attention to? Consider the following 6 points:

○ **Prepare.** Figure out what "stuff" you need to get creative and stay creative. Are you having a family craft fest? Movie night? Puppet show? Mini-triathlon? Art show? Meal-making session? Game night? Gather what's necessary, and make the experience fun from the start.

○ **Reflect.** Be willing to muddle through issues and extend thoughts with one another.

○ **Accept challenge.** Progressively tackle higher-level ideas. You'll likely have to work at this, like climbing rungs on a ladder or ridges on a rock face. Let others assist you if need be.

○ **Stay fresh.** Participate in different kinds of learning and experimentation. Pursue your own interests, *and* check out others' interests, too. You may be surprised where they lead. (This relates to what I said earlier in this chapter about the importance of appreciating one another's individual differences.)

○ **Use collective brainpower.** Tap your intellect and the knowledge of those close to you. Find, share, elevate, and preserve what's meaningful. In her book, *Little Things Long Remembered*, author Susan Newman writes about the importance of family activities and togetherness, and she says, *Starting traditions and making memories is much easier than you may think.*

○ **Advocate for one another.** This might include discussing plans to connect with your teachers so they can better support your creative abilities, curiosities, and strengths, and align your learning processes at school with those you're engaged with and developing at home.

The bottom line is that you and your family can play, learn, grow, and create together. You can buoy one another's efforts, confront trials, and navigate uncertainties. You can go on real and virtual explorations (check out *National Geographic Kids* magazines for cool ideas), and make endless discoveries across fields of study. Whenever you exercise your right to create uncharted ways forward through exploration, revision, or the juggling and extension of ideas, you open doors to excitement, personal growth, skill-building, and family fun. That can be wonderful!

Top Take-Aways from Chapter Four

- Your family is an important network for encouraging and reinforcing your efforts. There are endless possibilities for helping one another develop ideas, enjoy activities, and strengthen creative expression.

- Three practical ways family members can nurture and support your creativity are:

  ○ by working together to *promote life balance*—including a heathy daily mix of calm, busyness, and technology that empowers wellness

  ○ by *appreciating individual differences*—recognizing and respecting your individuality

  ○ by *being proactive*—taking initiative, for example by building upon accomplishments, sharing thoughts, and seeking and finding new experiences.

- You can help your family nurture and support your personal growth and creativity by strengthening connections with those whom you love and trust. Welcome their input, and be creative together. Let them know what makes you tick, including what you might need in order to prepare, develop reflective habits of mind, accept challenge, stay fresh, fortify your brainpower, and advocate effectively.

- When families play, learn, explore, and create, they grow stronger as a result—individually, collectively, and over time.

CHAPTER 5

Do You Struggle with Creativity? Reasons and Remedies

*The worst enemy to creativity is*_____.
I invite you to fill in the blank, and then continue reading.

The Perplexing Side of Creativity

You probably already know the upside of creativity. It can be fun, exciting, motivating, and help you solve thorny problems.

However, what if you find it difficult to "be creative" or to do things in an imaginative way? Maybe you don't want to put forth the time, patience, or effort that creative expression often requires. Or perhaps you don't like the "unknown" aspects of creative ventures, and would rather take a path of less resistance.

These are real reasons why kids struggle with creativity or choose to avoid it. We'll touch upon *many* reasons, and we'll look at some remedies, too.

For instance, what if you don't feel comfortable expressing yourself through art, poetry, music, drama, or some other means because you lack confidence in that particular area, or you don't think you're knowledgeable or capable enough in that domain.

By way of example, (and in relation to the fill-in-the-blank above) poet Sylvia Plath wrote, *The worst enemy to creativity is self-doubt.*

You may not agree. But at the time she wrote that, she was trying to decide whether to take a summer writing course at Harvard University or return home. She went home. Nonetheless, the important thing was that she overcame doubts and continued to work on her creative expression, and her writing flourished.

What if *you* experience self-doubt about doing something creative in one or more areas? What can you do?

You could start by pausing to collect your thoughts, and by thinking about what you know, and what you can do well. You could figure out how you might apply the knowledge, strengths, or skills that you already have, and polish or extend them in a new or innovative way—taking just one step, and then possibly continuing onward. You could share your uncertainty and your ideas, and collaborate with family and friends, and ask for their support, assistance, or guidance. You could reflect upon times you've succeeded before (and why), and how you might rekindle those sparks. You could focus on staying calm because creativity is largely about fresh originality, and there's no pre-set right or wrong, and no limits to possibilities. You could stop comparing yourself to others, or fretting if what you do is not exemplary or exact, or might even seem peculiar. Just be your own best self.

Psychologist Katie Hurley is the author of *The Stress-Busting Workbook for Kids*, and she writes often about children's and teens' emotions, coping strategies, and self-care. She says that everyone struggles with their feelings sometimes, and that feelings, thoughts, and needs are all interconnected. Her advice: *When you replace your inner critic with an inner cheerleader, you learn to give yourself praise and positive responses to your hard work.* You can unleash your mind, positivity, imagination, spirit, and potential!

But the paragraphs you've read in this chapter so far reflect an overview of just one set of circumstances (that is, self-doubt), and *one* collection of suggestions for confronting it—and then welcoming creativity.

Uncertainty, and a lack of confidence in some area(s), can emerge in the context of other reasons why people sometimes struggle with creativity. I discuss many of these below, and each is accompanied by some brief strategies to get through or around the difficulties. The ten headings that follow reflect several underlying causes why kids may not be as creative as they'd like to be. Keep in mind that suggestions that apply to one underlying cause might also work to mitigate another for you. So, stay openminded and consider taking note of whatever jumps out as a possible way to resolve a struggle you might be experiencing—and thereby increase your creativity.

Struggles: Reasons and Remedies

⚘ Scrutiny

Nobody likes it when people peer over their shoulder and tell them what to do or how to do it. That kind of "watch dog" situation is understandably nerve-wracking, intrusive, and annoying, and it can suppress or spoil a person's creative energy.

Remedies: Some individuals *like* having their activities overseen. However, if you find scrutiny stifling or disruptive then politely ask the "scrutineer" to give you some time and space. Explain that you're trying to think and work things through, and although you realize they have good intentions, you'd prefer to figure out matters on your own. Keep calm. You can show appreciation for their interest, listen to their comments, convey thanks, and then hold your ground by requesting they ease their supervision.

Courtesy is really important though. If you say "back off" or "go away" it may come across as harsh. You have the power to de-escalate a potentially prickly situation by being respectful, choosing your words carefully, and keeping your voice pleasant. You could also indicate a willingness to share what you're creating at a later point in time, perhaps once you're further along in your efforts. That kind of offer reflects compromise, showing that you're considerate of someone else's watchful eye and desire to be helpful, and accepting of it—albeit on your terms.

⚬ Stuck in a Rut

Do you get jammed up doing stuff? Are you hesitant to try a new approach or to look at an activity with a fresh or growth mindset? Do you like things to be the same as before, or "just so?" Then you may be rigid in your outlook. It's useful to have set routines and familiar ways of doing things. There's a comfort level to that. However, being stuck (like getting mired in quicksand) is not productive, and rigidity does not bode well for creativity either. Individuals who are inflexible in their thinking (that is, rigid), are less inclined to push past established limits and boundaries.

Remedies: It can be hard to stretch outside comfort zones, and if things are going well why mess with that? There's an old expression, *Why rock the boat?"*Simply put, those who are content to sail steadily in familiar waters may make progress and feel secure—but if they don't "rock" the norm, venture into new places, and try different experiences, they may miss out on exciting opportunities. Poet William Butler Yeats wrote, *The world is full of magic things, patiently awaiting for our senses to grow sharper.*

Take time to appreciate various options for pushing yourself, or sharpening your senses, a little at a time. A single sight, sound, or experience can trigger the stirrings of a creative idea (and you never know when that might occur). Creative individuals recognize the value of engaging meaningfully with what's around them, and then extending that engagement further. For example, let's say you're out for a walk. There's lots to see—above, below, in front, behind… Don't just walk. Make it an *wonderment* walk where you take time to both observe and wonder about what's around you. Activate your senses. Breathe in the smell of flowers and wet leaves; touch the texture of tree trunks; listen to birds loudly chirping and insects quietly droning; taste raindrops on the tip of your tongue; notice the lacey patterns atop frozen puddles on the sidewalk. You can share your experiences, and maybe record them with photos, by jotting ideas in a notebook, or drawing images. Find the unfamiliar within the familiar. Canadian artist and teacher Susan Gurau often shared insights like these with her students, and helped them to appreciate the wonders of each day. She emphasized the value of learning to focus. She said, *Seeing is often perceived by the creative mind. But seeing takes effort.* (More on effort in Chapter 7.)

In the book *Sky Color*, author Peter Reynolds reveals the importance of looking beyond what's expected (such as a blue sky), keeping your mind open, and seeing the world anew. And, comedian and entrepreneur Kevin Hart cautions against *staying in a small box with a small mindset.* So, hoist yourself up from any rut, dust off any lingering staleness from being stuck, and fire up your creativity!

♦ Impatience

When you're excited about something, you may be inclined to rush through it. Conversely, if you lack enthusiasm, you may want to "cut to the chase" and just get it over with. Either way, you might get careless. Patience involves waiting, persisting, and investing time and effort, whereas impatience is quite the opposite, and may involve rushing, tuning out, avoiding things, or directing your focus elsewhere. Creativity can be bolstered by patience, and it can be jeopardized by impatience.

Remedies: Impatience may look like frustration, intolerance, or disinterest. If impatience causes you to hurry through tasks, or turn away from them, pause and take stock of how you're responding, and why. You may prefer something to evolve quickly—even immediately—but think about how growth and development occur. Over time! You might have to learn to pace yourself or wait. Steps forward are good, yet steps backward or sideways can also be helpful and provide you with new perspectives, and ways of adapting to change. You can give yourself a pep talk, and say to yourself that you're *not* going to rush, slacken efforts, or give up, and then concentrate on deliberately following through on that. It might be inspiring, too, to consider the experiences of people whose accomplishments are borne of patience and hard work—for example, artists, athletes, doctors, actors, architects, astronauts, and teachers. They're not too hasty or impulsive. You, too, can ease up on impatience, and take pleasure in methodically doing what it takes to get to where you want to be.

One additional thought—sometimes what appears to be impatience is really something else. Like lack of sleep, needing to move or do something physical, being upset about a disagreement with a friend, or not doing well on a test. These kinds of occurrences may translate into what seems like impatience (or contribute to it), and can make you less inclined to do things. It's helpful to give careful thought to what might be underlying any edginess, avoidance, or displeasure that you might be experiencing, and that might masquerade as or lead to impatience. Awareness is the first step to resolving the problem. (Try to be patient when figuring it out.)

◊ **Complexity** ("too muchness")

When things get complicated it can be a turn off. Having to deal with too much at once can lead to confusion and/or feeling overwhelmed. Breaking down the complexity of a tough task can demand considerable concentration and effort, and therefore it may be a stretch to engage in creative expression as well.

Remedies: Complexity comes in different guises. Three examples: families have times of chaos and challenge; you have to navigate twists and turns if you're going to become adept at riding a bike; and learning new skills inevitably means climbing a series of escalating steps in order to increase ability levels. People confront complexity all the time.

The best way to manage complexity depends on the circumstances. Perhaps it means communicating openly and honestly with family members; slowing down when a route is circuitous or tricky; or carefully going ahead, bit by bit. You can try chunking matters of complexity into small manageable segments. For instance, if a book report assignment is too demanding, divide it into portions and tackle them one at a time so they're not such a burden, and so you can more readily use your imagination. You might create an interesting but straight-forward storyboard, or scaffold ideas from a framework that's already familiar to you.

Sometimes the world itself feels complex and overly stimulating. We can be inundated by all the sights, sounds, smells, and textures which provide incredible potential for growth and opportunities for the imagination to take wing, but that can also be overwhelming for many people. Have you ever heard of a *rainforest*? It's an outdoor environment teeming with different sensory experiences and life forms, all existing collectively in one place. Author and psychotherapist Paula Prober says that each person's mind is like a rainforest environment. How? She suggests that an individual's thinking and understandings are intertwined with the heart, soul, body, and spirit—similar to an ecosystem that must work together to flourish. However, ecosystems can be complex and overpowering, and some kids have trouble dealing with heightened ways of interacting with the intricacies of their surroundings, including intensified sensory exposure, or the many demands of daily life.

If that's something you experience, perhaps occasionally or even often, strategies you can consider include embracing your sensitivities, self-soothing through deep breathing techniques, and trying to accept and limit yourself to what you can manage comfortably. Psychologist Tina Harlow suggests greeting the world with *calm curiosity*—that is, taking the time and space you need to just let yourself feel okay. Harlow says it's important to listen to and honor yourself over any external hubbub, complexity, overload, or expectations, and to make meaningful connections (what she calls *building a village*) with others whom you trust. They can help you to feel good, and to find steady footing as you journey forth—thoughtfully and creatively, whether independently or together.

◉ Simplicity ("not enoughness")

Simplicity is the opposite of complexity. When something is too easy or not stimulating enough it can also interfere with your desire to be creative. You may tune out or be reluctant to try something original. You may have a "ho-hum" or "why bother?" attitude, and a lack of enthusiasm.

Remedies: If you're confronting a simple task, or perhaps one that's boring, think of it as an opportunity. What can you do to give a hum-drum activity some pizazz? How can you make it more interesting, exciting, or motivating? Creativity to the rescue! For instance, going back to the example of having to do a book report, if it's dreary or basic you can liven it up by complementing it with a gameboard, colour-ful illustrations, or a video. Be resourceful and try a new tech-based approach, use rhyme, or discover more about the author's life or other publications. You can also collaborate with friends, or brainstorm ideas. Or have a peek at how various authors format or add to stories in different or creative ways. A great example of this is Jeff Kinney's *Diary of a Wimpy Kid* books. (The latest in the series, number 18, is "*Diper Overlode*"). These books have funny sketches, atypical formats and font, interesting word choice, and amusing characters—and to date over 275 million of these stories have been sold! You, too, can upscale a story, writing assignment, or any other activity by choosing to make it somewhat unusual, witty, or unconventional. Why be conforming if you can be creative?

♨ Embarrassment

Some kids become concerned thinking that their creative products are not as good as someone else's, or worry that they could be laughed at or ridiculed for coming up with something silly, outrageous, or odd. Creativity is reflective of original or offbeat ideas, so creating an unusual work of art or innovative product is part of that. However, it can be challenging to be creative when feeling doubt, when hearing contrary or belittling comments from other people, or when won-dering if humiliation is just around the corner.

Remedies: If you have an idea that you want to explore, don't let yourself get bogged down worrying about what other people might think or say. What if you wanted to create cupcakes using pickles? Or choreograph underwater dance routines? Or decorate an entire doll house with glass mosaic pieces? Some people might be critical or think those ambitions are weird. That's *their* problem—not yours. In fact, there are several interesting pickle cupcake recipes, highly acclaimed synchronized swimming teams, and beautifully crafted mosaic homes of all shapes and sizes. Stick with your intent. Those who take inspiration to next levels may have to tune out doubters, negative vibes, or hecklers, however in the end there's satisfaction in creating something unique. Actress Zendaya says, *There are so many great things in life, why dwell on negativity?* Although your ideas may not suit everyone, that's okay. Creativity is about choice. Hey, not everyone likes pineapple pizza, country music, or quilting—but those who do will tell you that sloughing off or disregarding putdowns enables them to take pleasure in what they choose to enjoy.

It also helps to share ideas and hang out with people who have similar interests or who have an upbeat and creative spirit, and who will accept and encourage your preferences, efforts, and originality—as you accept and encourage theirs. Resolve to seize your moments and opportunities!

◊ Distractions

A distraction can cause you to veer off course or lose focus. Distractions can take the form of electronic devices, other people, cute puppies, flickering lights, doorbells, or anything that commands and sidelines your attention. Distractions come in all sizes, can assault the senses, may be unexpected, and are sometimes unavoidable (like tornadoes, and power outages). Distractions can forestall, interrupt, and derail your creativity.

Remedies: Think about what distracts you, and consider making a list. Online games? Snacks? Music? You could track how often distractions intrude, and try to reduce the frequency. Can you schedule them in so you can still enjoy them, but without interfering with your creativity or productive intentions? Then distractions can be like a break, giving you positive energy and a fresh start so you can reapply yourself. The duration of the break is yours to decide. For example, perhaps you feel distracted by a need to stretch or to do a physical activity from time to time. That's okay. Slot it in, and then resume what you were doing.

If you can, try to be mindful when working on things; that is, try to stay in the moment. You can practice paying attention to the here-and-now to avoid being distracted. You can learn more about mindfulness at your convenience. There's an abundance of courses, online programs, videos, interactive games, exercises, and books that describe different mindfulness techniques and activities that you can try.

Another tip is to work on your time management skills. You can find apps, agendas, and various instructional guides on how to use time wisely, set sensible limits, prioritize, and plan with an overall sense of direction—including carving out time to schedule those breaks, and practice mindfulness.

Worries can also be very distracting. For example, being afraid that you might fail at something can cause you to veer off course or stop you in your tracks, and thereby affect your productivity, enthusiasm, and creativity. Actress Emma Watson (who portrayed wizarding whiz Hermione Granger in the Harry Potter movies) says, *I don't want the fear of failure to stop me from doing what I really care about.* Similarly, versatile musician and rapper Nicki Minaj weighs in on fear. She advises (rather creatively), *You should never be afraid to become a piece of art. It's exhilarating.* Resolve and gumption can help to thwart fear and propel your momentum. Seeing mistakes and failures as chances to start over can also be productive. However, if fear of failure is a distraction, or troubles you, it's wise to speak to your parents and teachers about it. (*The Gift of Failure* by Jessica Lahey is an informative family resource book.) It's good to try and address fears or worrisome issues early on before they grow and fester, and possibly become even more distracting or troublesome.

Many of the struggles discussed within this chapter (such as scrutiny, being stuck in a rut, impatience, embarrassment, self-doubt, and more) can also be distracting. Whether you're distracted by desirable temptations, or undesirable disturbances or worries, becoming *aware* of what distracts you is a good starting point for dispelling the interference.

☙ Lack of Provisions

Creators create with "stuff." Materials may include paints, musical instruments, beads, fabric, chalk, and so on. It's smart to be prepared. If you have to scramble around to acquire the supplies you need to pursue your interests, then you end up wasting time, energy, and incentive, and creativity will wane.

Remedies: What exactly do you need? How can you get it? Who can assist you? How can you stay well-organized so that you have things like resource books and tech devices readily at hand? Who can you think of who can share stuff with you (including ideas), and how can you share with them? Moreover, consider how you might be able to embark on a creative project or proceed even if you can't get precisely what you want or need.

Author J. K. Rowling wrote the first Harry Potter book (*Harry Potter and the Philosopher's Stone*) on notepapers while sitting in a restaurant, sipping a single beverage, day after day after day. She didn't have much money to live on, but she was determined to write and release the fullness of her creativity! Turns out that what she really needed to be creative (aside from paper and pens), was desire, hard work, patience, imagination, resourcefulness, determination, and faith in herself. Depending on what people want to achieve, everyone's needs are different. Figure out yours, so you can be creative!

☙ Little or No Progress

It's heartening to see growth, whereas it's discouraging to experience lack of advancement. When you enjoy something, you feel motivated, and that's great. But what if you don't see actual progress? That can threaten your creative expression.

Remedies: Progress can take various forms, such as the *resolution* of a problem; feelings of *pride* about an artistic accomplishment; or taking a *next step* (such as moving from one musical instrument to another, or one material to another like paper to canvas, or play dough to clay). Sometimes progress is reflective of attaining a goal, but it can also be represented by gradual forward movement or improvement experienced along the way.

Instead of focusing on reaching a result, you can focus instead on your growth process—that is, the small bits that, when put together over time, become a meaningful whole. If you don't see progress yourself, you can always ask others to provide you with some feedback. You can also think back to some of your accomplishments, and appreciate how you made progress that may have not been evident at the time but nevertheless added up. Progress is about advancement but try not to be discouraged if it's slow.

⚭ Perceived Risk

People often avoid trying something if it appears risky. This can include creative activities. For example, think of dancers or gymnasts executing intricate moves, or actors doing precarious stunts. Safety can be a concern. In such circumstances, it makes good sense to carefully consider the extent and nature of any danger and, if need be, to back off. However, individuals who won't take a risk sometimes may never know how much they might accomplish. Poet T. S. Eliot wrote, *Only those who will risk going too far can possibly find out how far one can go.* Unfulfilled potential can be a direct consequence of being risk averse. Are you typically timid or brave? Why?

Remedies: T. S. Eliot's words about taking a risk may ring true, but nevertheless *going too far* may be foolhardy or reckless. Danger should be avoided. Unfortunately, it's not always obvious. Other times, it's apparent.

Risk can loom large, and sometimes it seems scarier, or more dangerous, or bigger than it really is. It's helpful to determine if a situation is *low-risk* (requires taking a chance but isn't perilous) or *high-risk* (can threaten your health or well-being). What's the evidence? Can you make the situation less risky? It also helps to determine the *importance* of doing the activity. Is it necessary? Enticing? A whim? Are others depending on you? Can you be careful?

If you want to be creative but you're struggling with the idea that it could be a risky undertaking, here are a few tips:

- ○ Get to know your capabilities, and build upon those. Take extra time to strengthen your knowledge and skills because increased know-how can reduce risk.

- ○ Have a friend or someone you can depend on help you out by providing guidance, advice, or reassurance, or by sharing the load.

- ○ Read about strategies that others have used to manage or lessen risk.

- ○ Divide and conquer risk by starting with what makes you feel secure or comfortable—such as making sure you have the right safety equipment—and then pacing yourself.

- ○ Keep kindling your resolve as you proceed through and beyond a risk. Remember the words of Dwayne Johnson (The Rock), who said, *I've learned never to say never.* He may be very strong physically, but like the rest of us, he also has to figure out how to intelligently mitigate or work around risks so "nevers" become "maybes" or thoughtfully considered "possibilities."

- ○ Appreciate that many things worth doing require some risk— for example, making new friends, or singing or speaking in front of an audience—but each achievement is a chance to discover creative outlets.

- ○ Change the *concept of risk* to adventure, opportunity, or escapade. This can reinforce your desire and creativity. Enjoy the thrill, build your strengths, and rise above any deterrents.

And, Finally...

Shel Silverstein wrote the following poem in his book *Where the Sidewalk Ends.*

> *Listen to the MUSTN'T, child,*
> *Listen to the DON'TS*
> *Listen to the SHOULDN'TS*
> *The IMPOSSIBLES, the WON'TS*
> *Listen to the NEVER HAVES*
> *Then listen close to me—*
> *Anything can happen, child,*
> *ANYTHING can be.*

It may be difficult to listen to people's negative views. Others may try to detour or undermine your initiative, creativity, or desire. However, think of that as part of a learning curve. In the end, you are in charge of your own actions, creativity, and effort, as you work toward overcoming struggles. ANYTHING is possible.

Top Take-Aways from Chapter Five

⚶ There are many reasons why kids may struggle with creativity. Sometimes *feelings of doubt* or a *lack of confidence* in one's ability in one or more areas can be at the root of struggles. This can be caused by various issues.

⚶ In this chapter, there are descriptions of several ways in which creative expression can be compromised, along with suggestions to help kids get over the difficulties. Challenges that can lead to struggles include the following: *scrutiny, being stuck in a rut, impatience, complexity, simplicity, embarrassment, distractions, lack of provisions, little or no progress,* and *perceived risk*.

⚶ The "remedies" provided are starting points to help you get past the roadblocks. Recommendations that appear in one segment may also be effective for hurdling other struggles that you might encounter. Indeed, be openminded about how you can apply any or all of the strategies so you can be more creative!

CHAPTER 6

Feel the Burn! What Are the Best Environments for Creativity?

Brain science tells us that emotional safety sets the foundation for our ability to learn new things. This foundation of safety serves to enhance self-confidence and the ability to think "outside the box."

~Mona Delahooke

It's vital to feel safe. It's certainly a priority for meaningful engagement in activities, and for personal growth and well-being. Are there other necessities?

Environmental Factors

Each learning environment has its own distinctive features—and potential for challenges, too. Whether it's a beach, park, concert venue, gym, ice rink, backyard, train station, open air market, or other locale, assess the safety factors *and* the opportunities. (Ideally before you go too far out on a limb.)

This picture of a bald eagle and a *juvenile* (next page) was taken by my friend, nature photographer Garnet Rich. The environment is very different from that of your home, but it is nonetheless about nurturing. The parent is teaching the child to go out on that limb, and learn to soar. What do you think is being communicated by these two?

Communication between a parent and child is important for encouraging independence, instilling confidence, and ensuring an environment that's safe. Respect for a child's individuality also matters—a lot. Anthropologist Margaret Mead wisely noted, *Always remember that you are absolutely unique. Just like everyone else.*

Psychologist Mona Delahooke (who I cite above), provides a practical perspective on people's responses and actions. In her book, *Beyond Behaviors* she explains, *Our individual differences coupled with our experiences predict how we react to situations.* Our reactions have a bearing on our behavior, and on learning and creativity as well. But situations and environments vary. And how kids manage their surroundings and experiences varies, too.

I *could* make this chapter on best environments lengthy and complex. I *could* talk about the many **responsibilities** that kids have over time as they learn to become strong, and capable. About how the world is always **changing**, and the importance of being ready to roll with and adapt to that. About the countless **resources** that are at your disposal. About why education, knowledge, connectivity, and a yearning for **learning** can contribute to your advancement and creativity.

I *could* address all of that.

However, I'll make this chapter extremely short because although **responsibility**, **adaptation to change**, **resources**, and **learning** are integral to a "best environment," you will see these points elsewhere within this book. (And in many other places, too.)

So, in a nutshell, what IS the best environment for nurturing creativity?

The best environment is safe. It's empowering. ***It's anywhere that is flexibly responsive to your desires (what you need and want to know and do), and holds the promise of possibilities.***

President John F. Kennedy said, *Together, let us explore the stars, conquer the deserts, eradicate disease, tap the ocean depths, and encourage the arts and commerce.* Those possibilities are endless—and creativity can transpire anywhere!

That said, the best environment is both respectful of, and open to, your ideas, choices, questions, and uniqueness. It's where you can connect with others and share thoughts and aspirations, and develop exciting new ones. It's welcoming, and comfortable. It enables you to fulfil your sense of purpose. It fosters your curiosity and invites you to embark on journeys, tackle challenges, take your time, and explore outlets ranging from the arts, to technology, to areas of interest that are so original or ground-breaking they may not even have existed last week. Explorations may be through nature (green spaces, parklands, forest trails, riverbeds); through face-to-face encounters (with first responders, mentors, seniors, athletes); through play (dress-up, spontaneous activities, role-play, games); and through arts and crafts (puppetry, scrapbooking, sewing, pottery).

The wider the range of opportunities available in the environment in which you find yourself—or choose to extend—over the course of your life, the greater the likelihood that you'll discover and take part in meaningful creative experiences. And, thereby set your world ablaze!

That's it!

End of chapter.

Beginning of creativity!

Top Take-Aways from Chapter Six

🔥 The best environment for nurturing creativity is one that invites you to explore different kinds of experiences and opportunities, and that empowers you to fulfill your desire to express yourself as you wish.

🔥 Responsibility, adaptation to change, resources, and learning all contribute to positive development.

🔥 If you're in a place where you feel safe, purposeful, and can engage in meaningful personal growth, you're likely to be more creative.

CHAPTER 7
Agency and Effort (Huh?)

In short, **agency** refers to action and involvement. **Effort** refers to work. They're interconnected. Creativity comes from taking responsibility for, and investing in, both agency *and* effort.

Many kids who are bright, capable, and achieve with considerable success in one or more areas, may nonetheless lack motivation, and the desire to put forth agency or effort. Some coast along. Some underachieve. Some worry about it. Some don't care. (Although their parents and teachers might.)

Lack of initiative can be a problem. Have you heard of the buzz word, "languishing?" It went viral after author Adam Grant wrote an article in 2021 for the *New York Times* suggesting that people are becoming less effortful. The title of the article was *There's a Name for the Blah You're Feeling: It's Called Languishing.*

Kids languish, too. Unfortunately, this tendency toward inactivity can have a direct and negative effect on attitudes, skill development, creativity, and engagement in learning.

There *are* times when people may opt to wind down or chill out, and this can be beneficial. We all like to relax on a couch or sit and do nothing sometimes. And many researchers, psychologists, and medical practitioners will attest to the fact that there are plenty of advantages to down-time (or being at ease if you please). For example, it's a chance to unwind, take stock of what's around you, think, read, decide about next steps, and play.

However, too much down-time, waning effort, and an avoidance of healthy challenges may not be beneficial, both in the short run and over the long haul.

Let's focus on **agency** first. Then we'll move on to **effort**, including how you can kickstart it, and how you can keep it going. Just so you know, I DON'T lecture about working hard, or what you should (or shouldn't) do. But I DO offer suggestions so you can take a better look at your agency and effort. Then you can decide if you'd like to use those suggestions to help fortify your attitudes and actions, and thereby fuel your creativity tank. Be cautioned, however, that as with many suggestions, these upcoming ones can involve changes, and (as indicated in Chapter 3) changes typically have an impact on outlook, behaviors, and outcomes.

About Agency

Planning, starting, and ultimately finishing a task may involve many steps. The process can go off the rails at any time—at the start, part way through, or nearing completion, as our daily lives have become increasingly hectic.

Many years ago, the brand Nike created a popular advertising slogan: *Just do it!* That message is still relevant. It conveys the power of being proactive and participating in experiences. You have that power. You just have to take ownership of it. Each individual decides what to settle on, what to put aside or avoid, and what to strive for on any given day.

What other powers contribute to agency? Here are a few:

○ **Agency and Hope**. Ancient philosopher Aristotle said, *Hope is a waking dream*. If that's true, that's probably good because fantastic things can happen in a dream! What do you hope to accomplish? How? What can you do first? What resources can you find? What technology might be useful? Who can you connect with (a mentor? a coach? a teacher? a grandparent?) to help make your dreams come true?

Cognitive psychologist Scott Barry Kaufman emphasizes the importance of *choosing growth,* believing in yourself and your dreams, and self-advocating—that is, speaking up for what you need to make them come true. He writes a lot about *self-actualization*—fulfilling your desires and becoming your best self. In a recent interview, Kaufman said *Sometimes we have this deep reservoir of agency we didn't even know we had.* So, think about your hopes, explore options, and follow your strengths, inclinations, and dreams.

○ **Agency and Life Balance.** Care for yourself. And regulate your activities so that you can comfortably manage the things you have to do. Find your sense of calm. Take time to play, to enjoy family time, to pause, to generate and then collect your thoughts. Think, too, about your achievements, and how to use, share, or extend them wisely—over time, and at a pace that suits you. (In Chapter 4, I discuss how your family can help to support your life balance.)

○ **Agency and Free Will.** Ian Rowe, is the author of the book *Agency.* He describes agency as *free will guided by a moral sense of right and wrong.* In writing about self-betterment, Rowe discusses the value of understanding the difference between what *is* in your life, versus what you want it *to be*. He says agency involves seeing ourselves as *architects of our own better futures,* and he suggests we *do so even in the face of real obstacles.* In other words, your will has a bearing on how your life will unfold.

However, Rowe also recognizes that connecting with others is important for fortifying will, for developing agency, and for advancing. Rowe recommends forging strong connections through family ties, school, community, religious institutions, and entrepreneurship.

○ **Agency and Past Experience**. (Retrospection.) Creativity expert Felice Kaufmann emphasizes the value of looking back upon meaningful experiences you've had or memorable situations you've been in, and reflecting specifically on your agency. How did you make good things happen? What motivated you? How did you draw out your strengths? What made you feel proud, or successful? Perhaps it had to do with being with friends, maximizing leisure or learning times, or something else. By understanding how your agency contributed to your happiness you can potentially embrace that approach again.

○ **Agency and Planning**. (Forethought.) Focus on what lies ahead, one step at a time. If you already know something, but don't know the *next* something, that could be a logical starting point. Plan to build from there. You can try an online planning app, use a visual action plan (like consulting a roadmap), or devise (and update) checklists to help you stay on track. Your past experiences, including plans that worked well, can also guide your way forward. Be sure to incorporate time for "catching up" or for revisions as part of your plan.

○ **Agency and Negotiation and Compromise**. These are two important and learnable skills. However, negotiation and compromise require flexibility—that is, a willingness to adjust (and sometimes readjust) your strategies, views, timelines, or whatever else requires tweaking as you proceed. Be open to talking with others, and to meeting them halfway. Arguing is counterproductive. Cool heads prevail. Musician Taylor Swift wrote, *Anytime someone tells me that I can't do something, I want to do it more.* It's great to want to prove things to yourself and to others, but do so respectfully and with negotiation and compromise as warranted.

○ **Agency and Time, Place, Feelings, and Circumstance**s. There may be certain times of day and year when you feel more energized; certain places that inspire you more than others; certain feelings that get your creative juices bubbling;

and certain people and situations that make you more inclined to get moving. You might want to consider these, and their impact on you. One by one, think about how you can maximize those times, places, feelings, and circumstances so you can make the most of them.

About Effort

> *If you want to be the best version of yourself,*
> *don't settle for being less, doing less, or learning less.*
> *It will compromise your intelligence, wellness,*
> *and creativity, and impede your productivity.*

Those words appear in a resource I wrote entitled *Productivity Through Adversity.* I share the quote here because it's about the importance of effort. There are many reasons why effort matters, only one of which is that it will boost your creativity. After you read through the seven points below, consider chatting about them with your parents to see if they agree, and how they might be able to assist you. You might even want to get creative and debate these ideas, going back and forth over them. (Heads up, it will involve critical and divergent thinking, and it'll require effort—but that's okay!)

- ○ **Effort helps desires come true.** What you aspire toward is not always attainable, depending on the *size* of your aspirations, how *reachable* they might be, and what *supports* you have in place. For example, If you'd like to learn to play piano, you'll need a keyboard and some instruction. If you enjoy painting, you'll require art materials. Those are basic practicalities. They're not hugely demanding. Ultimately though, hopes and dreams are intensified by effort as well as practicalities. Aspirations are great starting points, but if you want to turn possibilities into accomplishments it will require preparation, self-discipline, and hard work. Be *proactical*— that's my personally invented descriptor for being proactive *and* practical. Do you have a favorite author, dancer, role model...? Explore how they *proactically* strove to succeed.

○ **Effort is a learning curve.** Effort leads to better understandings of what you can do well, what you might have to work harder on, and what kinds of help you might need to rise above difficulties. That's a learning curve. For example, you may decide you want to have more of a positive attitude, or develop stronger math skills, or increase your autonomy, or have access to certain resources to complete something you choose to do. Figuring those things out—including steps for attaining them—can be very helpful in marshalling effort and moving ahead. Your learning curve is uniquely yours, but thinking about and validating understandings relating to your abilities will help to fortify your effort.

○ **Effort leads to greater confidence.** Support your efforts by congratulating yourself on your steps forward—small ones, big ones, and the ones in between. Take pride in your successes as they occur. The truth is that you may feel more competent and confident in some areas than others. For example, you may be really great at building structures like sandcastles, but not so great at dancing. Kids can have different levels of confidence for different dimensions of their lives—academic, social, athletic, and so on. And, that's to be expected.

Factors that may have a bearing on your confidence include your thoughts about previous successes, perceived degree of risk, and your resilience in the face of difficulties. Perhaps most important is the belief that, with effort, you can succeed. If you pay attention to those factors, you will gain confidence!

○ **Effort furthers creative and intellectual development.** It's smart to take advantage of learning experiences in different areas, and over time. When you find relevant pursuits, develop them further by honoring them, and by investing effort because this will help you progress. You empower yourself when you expand your range of skills and knowledge—and this, in turn, increases your base for creative expression. It's like standing on a sturdy foundation as you try to reach upward.

Billionaire entrepreneur Mark Cuban said, *Talent without effort is wasted talent. And while effort is the one thing you can control in your life, applying that effort intelligently is next on the list.* Effort can lead to intelligence, but the concept that effort should be used intelligently is both sensible and though-provoking.

○ **Effort leads to collaboration with others.** If you get started on a task or activity, try to make connections as you proceed. Having others on-side can help foster and support your efforts, and this can lead you toward accomplishments and qualities that you can feel good about. It's good to strengthen your relationships with friends, family, community members, and others you trust and with whom you share similar interests.

○ **Effort increases engagement and independence.** If you have a take-charge attitude, you will achieve more. Think about riding a horse. If you firmly take the reins, it'll be a smoother ride than if you don't. So, for example, you could resolve to learn chess, steer a kayak, complete a difficult thousand-piece puzzle… Opportunities abound. Select one. Or two. Take control, put forth effort, and you'll experience satisfaction as well as greater independence. (Again, this has to do with *self-actualization*.) In fact, you might even consider doing something you might not normally do, something that may be outside your comfort zone. You could try one or more unusual foods or drinks; visit a museum and spend time focusing on a topic that you know absolutely nothing about; or participate in a sport that you've never tried before. You might discover a whole new side of yourself!

○ **Effort boosts brainpower (neural plasticity and the brain's developmental pathways).** It's helpful to learn about how your brain works, and what creative and other advantages can come from effortful brain-building activities such as problem solving, exploring, tackling new skills, and preparing thoughtfully for various possible outcomes.

No matter how old, or bright, or well-supported you might be, some things in life will inevitably prove challenging. It's best if you can learn how to muster effort for whenever you might require it. Effort affects every aspect of life including your schooling, what happens at home, your thoughts, your feelings, your extracurricular activities, and your community involvement. There are lots of opportunities therein to nurture effort. Look for people who can encourage you.

Also, here's a tip that you might not have considered. Be wary of *convenience*, and try not to let it interfere with your opportunities to extend or exert yourself. Focusing on what's close by, readily accessible, or immediate can be handy and beneficial but it might also be limiting. For example, if you live in a city or town, and you and your family want to gaze at constellations, you could find a spot outside where it's convenient to look skyward at night. However, bright lights can interfere with the number of stars you're able to see. If you go into the countryside where it's much darker, star gazing becomes a totally different experience. You'll be able to see many more stars and constellations. Taking that effortful step, and pushing yourself beyond what's easy or close, may be more inspirational. In other words, what's less opportune may be more opportune!

You can complement or add to what's convenient for you, and at the same time elevate your creativity. Try to visualize how to go past the here-and-now as you reflect upon and pursue your aspirations. What's seems appealing or interesting? You could find an online mentor *across the globe*; cook up dishes with herbs or vegetables *that you grow yourself*; build a tree fort *with special architectural effects* as opposed to a typical structure. According to the Oxford dictionary, convenience is *the state of being able to proceed with something with little effort or difficulty*. An activity that's easy, nearby, or relatively effortless may not be as gratifying as it could be. Convenience may be limiting rather than fulfilling.

Fulfillment and effort meld together like macaroni and cheese. The best way you can learn about the value of effort is by engaging in your own fulfilment!

But don't put it off.

How to Enhance Agency and Effort

I wrote a book entitled *Bust Your BUTS*. Within that book, I describe issues having to do with putting things off (*procrastination*), including what can cause that. Some reasons are *personal*. For example: not caring enough, being bored, not feeling well, being confused, fearing failure, or being lazy. Other reasons for avoiding doing stuff are *skill-related*. These might include being disorganized, or having difficulty with decision-making, prioritizing, planning, setting goals, or time-management. Reasons for procrastination may also be *external*, such as distractions, having pesky people around, being confronted with too many technological demands, or not having the necessary materials. I wrote *Bust Your BUTS* for kids who procrastinate, but many of the recommendations for overcoming avoidance behavior also apply to kids who may need help with *agency* (involvement) and *effort* (work). I also wrote *Not Now, Maybe Later: Helping Kids Overcome Procrastination*. Although it's mainly for parents and teachers, you can read that book as well. (Maybe later?)

In the meantime, here are a few suggestions. They align with the tips that I share in those books.

○ **Find your sweet spot**. Eating something sweet, like candy, makes me happy. It also gives me a burst of energy so I can get things done (like completing this book), *and* be creative. In other words, candy (in my case chocolate) is motivating. Sometimes someone's motivational strategy may seem amusing, weird, or unexpected. Or it may be right or motivating for one person but not for another. What's your sweet spot?

○ **Push yourself.** You won't know your limits, or what you can do, until you try. So, why not try? Thomas Edison invented the filament light bulb. It demanded agency and effort. Edison said, *Our greatest weakness lies in giving up. The most certain way to succeed is always to try just one more time.* He made around 1000 attempts and did lots of guesswork before he succeeded with his light bulb. (Thankfully he kept at it!)

○ **Start.** One step. Just one. Then another... The beginning is the most important phase of action because it's what gets you moving forward. Check off steps as you proceed. This will help you to see your progress. Philosopher Lao Tsu wrote, *A journey of a thousand miles must begin with a single step.*

○ **Simplify.** Confusion is an inevitable part of life, but you can get through it by breaking things down into smaller or manageable components. Many florists create beautiful arrangements from workbenches piled with blooms, twigs, and ribbons. Writers (myself included) often have desks strewn with notes and papers. Chefs have pantries and counter tops loaded with assorted ingredients. But these creators pare down the stuff to what they actually need—bit by bit, as they embrace their creative energy. Mathematician Isaac Newton wrote, *Truth is ever to be found in simplicity, and not in the multiplicity and confusion of things.* That said, there's something about messiness that's appealing, fun, and when combined with agency and effort, may also lead to marvellous and creative outcomes!

○ **Set or co-set reasonable expectations**. Reasonable expectations are *fair*; that is, they're doable, and they're suitably targeted to your ability level so that you'll feel satisfaction and a sense of accomplishment upon attaining them. Fairness may hinge on what you're willing to do, and how much time, involvement, and effort you're willing to invest. It makes good sense to participate in co-creating expectations, thereby ensuring that they're appropriate. In *Bust Your BUTS* I wrote, *It's motivating when others expect good things from you. However, what's really important are the expectations that you have for yourself, based on what comes from within, and what you think is reasonable.*

If you take ownership of your activities through agency and effort, you'll be more inclined to commit to them and to see them through. Seek guidance if you have difficulty, consider how you can use various resources, and fortify your strengths as well as any areas of weakness. Encouragement and support from parents and teachers can also be very helpful, so reach out when necessary.

Teen entrepreneur and visionary Kevin Cooper was ambitious and self-assured. He wrote, *It isn't that my generation isn't capable. We just need the freedom, encouragement, and empowerment to show what we can do.*

Indeed, if you steer yourself well, and have faith in your abilities, you will be enroute toward doing whatever you set your mind to do. Plus, there are strategies that can help you optimize your creativity. You'll find 100 of these in the pages that follow.

Top Take-Aways from Chapter Seven

🔥 *Agency* and *effort* go together, and both contribute to creativity. Agency has to do with action (participation, involvement), and effort has to do with work (exerting yourself).

🔥 You can take ownership of agency by taking initiative, and by paying attention to the following considerations: hope; life balance; free will; past experiences; planning; negotiation and compromise; and the ways in which you make the most of various times, places, feelings, and circumstances.

🔥 Effort is valuable. It will help you to realize your desires; acquire a better understanding of what you can do; give you a greater sense of confidence; advance creative and intellectual development; enable more collaboration and relationship-building; increase engagement and independence; and boost your brainpower. However, don't let *convenience* get in the way of your taking full advantage of opportunities to exert yourself. Remember, being effortful leads to being fulfilled!

🔥 Procrastination is avoidance behavior (putting things off), and it can interfere with agency and effort. People have different (and legitimate) reasons for procrastinating. These reasons may be personal, skill-related, or external—however, there are many things you can do to overcome procrastination and apply yourself more wholeheartedly to tasks and activities.

🔥 Some strategies for "busting your buts" include finding what motivates you (your "sweet spot"), pushing yourself forward, focusing on that very first step, simplifying matters, and co-setting reasonable expectations. There are lots of other ways to overcome procrastination, and if you use agency and effort—and resourcefulness—you can discover these, experience the benefits, and ignite your creativity, too.

Section Three:
The Blaze You Choose

CHAPTER 8

100 Sure-Fire Ways to Ignite Your Creativity

You may have decided to go directly to this page to see the 100 strategies, thinking that you'll read the previous pages within this book another time. That's fine! But if that's the case, I hope you will check out the other chapters because there are LOTS of good suggestions in there.

This is intentionally and by far the longest chapter in this book. Inspiration can come from countless sources—people, places, and things; circumstances and experiences that foster reflection; or whatever you encounter that revs up your mind, feelings, or soul. The 100 suggestions described here can jump-start your ideas, and you can select which ones you might want to pursue.

Organizational Options

When you're reading through the many strategies, you might find it helpful to have a way to keep your thoughts organized. With that in mind, here is a quick approach you could try. As you discover suggestions that might work well for you, simply "ear mark" them with a little star inside the box. ★ (Or a tiny ear sketch 👂)

However, if you prefer a more considered approach, you could jot down one or more short form notations (or tags) in the margins beside any of the 100 items that catch your eye or tweak your imagination. I'm going to suggest three possible organizational schemes that will help you refer back to ideas at any time.

Organizational Approach #1

Here's the first possibility:
Use Tags A, B, C

- 🔥 **A—kindling the sparks**—if you want to *start* igniting some creative activities

- 🔥 **B—tending the flames**—if you want to "fan the fire," and *extend* your existing creativity

- 🔥 **C—turning up the heat**—if you want your creative inferno to *blast* full force

The abbreviations **A**, **B**, and/or **C** are convenient tags. So, when you revisit the pages later, the notations in the margins may help you decide which strategies to try, depending on whether you're interested in creative *sparks*, *flames*, or *blasts*.

Organizational Approach #2

Here's a second organizational scheme:
Use tags ONE, TWO, THREE

- 🔥 **ONE—in a flash**—if you want to use this creative idea *immediately*

- 🔥 **TWO—keep the glimmer**—if you want to think about using the idea *in a little while*

- 🔥 **THREE—let it smoulder**—if you want to put an idea on a "back burner" for *much later*

The tags are **ONE**, **TWO**, or **THREE**, and the key concepts are *flash*, *glimmer*, or *smoulder*. (Or now, soon, or eventually.)

Organizational Approach #3

Finally, this is a third possibility:
Use tags M, M+, F

🔥 **M—is for ME**—if it's something you'd like to do *on your own*

🔥 **M+—is for ME PLUS**—if it's something you think you'd like to do with *friends*

🔥 **F—is for FAMILY**—if it's an idea or activity that would be well-suited for your *family*

And here's a thought: You could attach **M**, **M+** and/or **F** to any of the other organizational options above—thereby mixing, matching, and firing up various possibilities for using the 100 strategies!

So, now you have several different handy organizational approaches to apply (if you so choose) as you read through the strategies—and you might even be able to think up another creative approach, or devise strategy numbers 101, 102, or 103. You decide how to proceed. This is your book, so make it work for you. (However, if it's a library book, please don't mess with the check boxes and margins. You can use paper or a tech file to record the emboldened words of any items that you want to keep track of, and still apply the same organizational approaches.)

You can jump around the following pages, or you can pick numbers randomly, or make a game of choosing them (with a friend or family member) and see what all the ideas are. I've inserted a few direct links within this particular chapter that you can copy into a browser, but don't forget that in the last section of this book you'll also find a list of handy resources and references to material from the other chapters, too.

Read on. It's a great way to fuel your creativity!

Starter Fuel and Heat Flashes

> *Go get your greatness!*
> ~Ronnie Rowe

Here are lots of incendiary ideas…

❑ **1. Read.** Reading is a portal to new worlds, past, present, and future, and wherever your imagination chooses to go. Sci-fi, historical fiction, cartoons, art, mystery, crafts, and how-to books—so many options, with diverse themes, fresh perspectives, problem-solving strategies, and more. Stories can spark new stories. Reading broadens understandings of the ordinary, the extraordinary, and everything in between. In a recent article I wrote, *Words are magical. They intertwine, collide, fuse, and reassemble, and with the push of a pen or the tap of a keyboard, they transform themselves into poetry, plays, lyrics, legends, memoirs, theories, fairy tales, and grand adventures.* Now that's creativity!

❑ **2. Share your ideas with those you trust.** If you let friends and family know about your aspirations and goals, and the steps you're taking to reach them, they can offer you encouragement, reassurance. suggestions, and maybe even provide points of view that haven't occurred to you yet. These people can be enthusiastic, becoming your own personal cheering squad that can help you increase your motivation and productivity. In his book, *I Used to be Gifted,* teacher Mark Hess uses the word *tailwinds* to refer to such people—but the term tailwinds can also apply to the situations, abilities, environments, and supports that empower you and enable you to soar. Your parents, teachers, extended family, classmates, mentors, and others can be tailwinds, and your strengths and creativity can be tailwinds, too.

❑ **3. Look to science.** Researchers have discovered that aromas can bring back very specific memories and associations, and that this could help to increase brain power. Simple exercise routines can also help enhance memory. These are just two small examples of research-oriented findings that, in turn, may spark exploratory ideas for you. What aromas? (Chicken soup? Chocolate fudge? Wet dog?) What kind of exercise routines? (Weightlifting? Water aerobics? Gymnastics?) What other research is happening around the brain—or the spine, heart, eyes, feelings, or other areas that have to do with the body or mind? Or maybe delve into a totally *different* area of science… What might *you* investigate? Get creative!

❏ **4. Promise yourself that you'll do something creative every day.** Then keep that promise. Try different initiatives—whatever *you* feel like. Poet E. E. Cummings enjoyed artistic freedom, and he loved to experiment with words, including grammar, inventive combinations, and punctuation. Between the ages of 8 and 22 he wrote a poem every day. That's over 5000 poems! (He wrote this: *completely dare/be beautiful*—which is good advice.) What might you be able to accomplish by this time next year if you try some kind of creative activity for 365 consecutive days? (You could pare it down to a month or a week if that's more manageable.)

❏ **5. Check out craft, hobby, and dollar stores.** What's interesting? Frames, flowers, foam? Wood, wires, wax? Beads, baskets, blocks? Paint, paper, pots? Clay, canvas, cork? See what attracts your attention, and consider what you might be able to do with it. Throw in some imagination for good measure. Publisher Molly Isaacs-McLeod wrote, *Creativity means more than crayons, glue, and glitter.* True—much more! But nevertheless, those items can be useful!

❏ **6. Up the ante on fun family time.** Spend more time doing creative activities with your family. Examples might be to have photo, karaoke, or baking challenges; tie-dye matching tee shirts or socks; plan an outing or day trip; devise different ways to make mealtime gatherings more stimulating; or get involved in family exercise sessions and game-playing activities. Or find different ways to be kind to others. For example, my niece, nephew, and their two daughters end each calendar year by posting a "50 days of kindness" challenge on social media. They share photos, suggestions, and information about how to spread kindness, one day at a time. How could your family promote kindness? (See Chapter 4 for many family-oriented opportunities to pursue.)

❑ **7. Make an "all about me" poster.** Include key words, images, or ideas that are important to you, such as goals you hope to reach, people you know or want to know, foods you like or want to try, places you've seen or hope to visit, and other things that reflect the real you. Hang the poster on your wall. Keep adding to it as you discover new interests and abilities, and as your networks continue to grow—and as you do. You can make "all about" posters for family members, too! They could make great gifts.

❑ **8. Network.** Use different supports and resources, community-based, or further afield, aloft, or afloat. Networking (building relationships) can help you stretch your learning parameters and your imagination. Find out about your family's and friends' networks, too. For example, in the 2022 movie, *The Fablemans* (based loosely on the early life of film director Steven Spielberg), the protagonist, Sam, is introduced to an older and experienced professional who shares some advice. The young aspiring filmmaker learns that showing a horizon at the bottom or at the top of a picture is *interesting*, whereas showing a horizon in the middle is *boring*. This tip helps Sam re-envision his efforts and hone his craft by changing how he views scenes, and how he might depict them creatively on film. Even a small bit of advice from someone in *your* extended network can turn out to be impactful!

❑ **9. Set clear expectations.** If you're muddled or confused about end-goals you won't feel as creative or as excited about trying to get there. Clarify what it is you want or have to do. (Those may be two very different things!) You can aim for the "target" but adjust if need be as you go along. Sometimes setting clear short-term or medium-term goals makes it easier to reach the long-range ones.

❑ **10. Compare, contrast, link...** Put things together in new ways. Try combining components, finding parallels, looking for similarities (or differences), and tying together (or pulling apart) unusual and even more unusual ideas. Lots of products were created by people who did just that! For example, you can buy shelves held up by suction cups, gloves with built-in flashlights or heaters, toaster bags, mopping slippers, and those popular magnetic phone mounts for use in cars or other places. This combines with that, and voila!

❑ **11. Write letters**. Create the stationery. Connect. With whom? How about relatives, friends, neighbors, people who have helped you in the past, or a famous person you admire?

❑ **12. Declutter.** Then have a garage, attic, or contents sale. Make colorful signs. Display things creatively. Price them out fairly. Use or donate profits wisely. And why not reimagine and redecorate the space you've decluttered? (You can also embrace clutter if you prefer, and repurpose items that you've accumulated to create something exciting. That could be fun!)

❑ **13. Interview individuals or groups who seek to make the world a better place.** For example, conservationists, or people who run charitable organizations. You could ask them when they're most creative. Who motivated them to succeed thus far? What do they look forward to? What are they working on now? What makes them happy? What can they teach *you* about being creative? And, how can you help?

❑ **14. Get entrepreneurial.** Check out television episodes of *Shark Tank Kids* by watching clips on YouTube, or read up on some of the young people who have designed products that are innovative. For instance, there's the children's silicone teething spoon, liquid bandage booboo glue, bee sweet lemonade, le-glue (for Lego), the touch-up cup paint container, and Mo's Bows.

❑ **15. Make a family scrapbook or family tree.** Use photos, mementos, cards, letters, drawings, documents, and other items. How far back can you go? Who can help you go further or lead you to discover destinations or events that you might not have known were a part of your family's history? How might knowing more about your ancestry inform your current perspectives?

❏ **16. Create a time capsule.** You can do this independently, or with others. Pick a container that will withstand time and potentially harsh conditions, and select a place to stash it. Decide what to put into the capsule, and set a date for a future opening. Then pull the plan together.

❏ **17. Volunteer in the community**. Perhaps you can help at the local playground, or join a youth group that addresses recycling, safety measures, or other pressing issues in your neighborhood. Or you could support a non-profit organization by donating your time and energy toward a good cause of your choosing.

❏ **18. Create an ABC book.** Settle on a theme. (Like exciting places in different countries, species of animals doing weird antics, or types of outrageously yummy or yucky desserts.) You can ask others to contribute ideas. You could make your book rhyme, or make it funny, or even have it go backwards—ZYX. Create illustrations and color them in. You can share your ABCs with little ones, and they can add to it. You can also create a 123 book, and have it go as high as you like.

❏ **19. Consider opposing viewpoints**. Get creative by considering other people's differing perspectives. Let your ideas bubble along by looking into topics of interest that may be controversial, or debatable, or that invite deliberation. For example, should dog owners be allowed to take their pets into grocery stores? Should cell phones be permitted at the dinner table? Should people be able to set off firecrackers in public parks? What do you think? Why? What might someone else think? Why? If there are problems raised, perhaps there are creative solutions.

❏ **20. Go crazy in the kitchen.** Bake and decorate. Make pasta or spaetzle from scratch. Braid a bread. Toss together an unusual salad. Create original recipes. Set a table that reflects a theme. Look for ways to use up stuff that's been sitting around in the cupboards or fridge for a while. Make "animals" or funny or scary faces with pancakes, chocolate chips, squiggly noodles, and candy eyes or mustaches. See what ideas appear in cookbooks, and in cake decorating books and videos, too.

❑ **21. Play your own version of "what if?"** Here are a few… What if a toadstool was actually a toad stool? What if a head of lettuce could think, or an ear of corn could hear, or the eye of a needle could see? What if a waterfall flowed backward, and the mouth of the nearby river could talk about it? What if boot camp was a camp for boots? What if you could come up with even more creative "what if" ideas?

❑ **22. Find your purpose.** Compassion? Optimism? Courage? Patience? What's important to you, and how might it affect your creativity? Think about it. Chat about it. In his recent book, teacher Mark Hess suggests 6 different avenues for exploring and extending whatever matters to you. You could: i) *perform or write* (plays, poems, speeches, songs….); ii) *draw or design* (brochures, slideshows, prototypes, props…); iii) *imagine* (anything!—and then demonstrate or communicate your thoughts…); iv) *calculate or measure* (maps, flowcharts, graphs, surveys…); v*) build or create* (models, games, mazes, scaled structures…); and vi) *discover more* (interview, read, experiment, and share your products or ideas).

Hess likes to create a three-dimensional six-face cube (similar to dice) that have each of those six options written on them. Then a roll of the cube provides an action plan or way forward. If the roll result is not your preference, you can take on the challenge anyways, or roll again for a different approach for pursuing in greater depth whatever is purposeful for you.

❑ **23. Read these three creativity-oriented books—plus others.** *The Dot, Ish,* and *Sky Color* are all by Peter Reynolds. They're about unexpected ways to get creative. There are some really old books, too, that contain terrific ideas. Don't overlook these! One of my favorites is *I Can Make A Rainbow* (by Marjorie Frank, published almost 50 years ago, in 1976). Ideas included in that book include: food and vegetable prints, mud art, salt sculptures, tablecloth decorating, batik, stencil tricks, oil swirls, sand candles, paper mâché masks, and windchimes. What other interesting old (or new) books can give *you* ideas? Ask people for their suggestions. You can also speak to a librarian.

❑ **24. Attune to your senses.** For example… *Smell* rain, stinky fish, spices, or roasted foods. *See* patterns in pavement, shadows in corners, patterns in snowflakes, or rainbowed sunlight through a prism. *Hear* birds, wind in branches, children's chatter, or rumbles in the sky. *Touch* what's rough, mushy, fuzzy, or spongy around your house or elsewhere. *Taste* what's sour, sweet, bitter, spicey, or salty. Take time to reflect upon creative ways to describe each of these things!

❑ **25. Make a collection.** Think rocks, seashells, or leaves. Or hair ornaments, candles, or action figures. You could gather items that are mysterious, glitzy, or bizarre. Exhibit your collection creatively. Continue to add to it over time, and perhaps make new collections.

❑ **26. Be creative, day by day.** For example, my friend Rina makes a colorful collage every Monday. (She posts pictures of it online to inspire others.) Tuesday is always fun food day at a local summer camp. A photographer I know focuses on nature images each Wednesday morning. Thursday is "theme day" at a nearby community day care center (and kids learn about specific colours, animals, or shapes). And Friday is costume day at the neighborhood library, and children are encouraged to dress up like a character in a storybook. What can you focus on—and build upon—regularly each week?

❑ **27. Read aloud to dogs in shelters.** (Or elsewhere.) Discover and recite poetry, role-play different voices, reread picture books you loved when you were younger. At the same time, you'll be making dogs happy. (Cats, birds, and turtles might be good listeners, too.) You can take pictures of you and your "audience" enjoying the readings, and share these photos with your friends to inspire them to read, and possibly also provide uplifting experiences for animals.

❏ **28. Interview someone who does something really unusual.** Dig deep into what they do, why they do it, and what drives their creativity by preparing thoughtful questions, asking them, and listening to the answers. Try to see the world through their eyes. Perhaps you could interview a store Santa, a juggler, a golf course designer, or...? Alternatively, record or write about a pretend conversation with an intriguing person from the present, past, or future. Or imagine chatting with a superhero, or an unusual character from one of your favorite books. What do they think? See? Feel? What can you learn from their experience, or by taking their viewpoints?

❏ **29. Let quotes inspire you.** There are lots of quotes throughout this book. (At the end, I've provided a list of all the people I cite.) I enjoy sharing comments that relate to or give emphasis to ideas I write about. I also find that inspirational quotes often provide new directions for creative thought, and help me take my ideas further. *Who seeks shall find* (Philosopher Sophocles).

Look up quotes from famous (or not so famous) people you admire, or whose life stories or accomplishments pique your curiosity. See if or how their words might inspire you. Check out *Brainy Quotes* at https://www.brainyquote.com online. Let the comments help you think creatively.

Pediatrician Marianne Kuzujanakis regularly and purposefully posts online what she calls *words that inspire*—quotes that she artistically displays (great idea!), and that she hopes will motivate others and contribute to their well-being. For example, she has shared these words by actor Charlie Chaplin: *You'll never find a rainbow if you're looking down.* And this advice, conveyed by author Annie Proulx, *You should write because you love the shape of stories and sentences, and the creation of different words on the page.* Words—written, spoken, signed, sung, or displayed—*are* inspiring!

❑ **30. Take an alternate route to wherever it is you usually go.** Plus take a different route on the return. Observe what's interesting. Choose an alternate route tomorrow. And the next day. New pathways provide new revelations.

❑ **31. Be crafty.** For example, create finger puppets relating to a fairy tale. Build a teddy bear. Make a Jillian Jiggs pig (see Phoebe Gilman's books); or a bus with wheels that go round-'n-round (as per the folk song written by Verna Hills); or a Very Hungry Caterpillar (as popularized by the book of the same name by Eric Carle). Keep the crafty outcome for your own pleasure, or give it to a young child. You can also share a song or a story to go along with it.

❑ **32. Surprise someone.** Do something nice but *totally* unexpected. Don't get too fussed about artistry or technique; it doesn't have to be anything jaw-dropping. Just focus on the interaction, and the way your creativity and thoughtfulness can strengthen the relationship.

❑ **33. Change the endings of stories you know and love.** You could make them funnier, scarier, or add new characters or situations. Or you could create prologues. That is, what happened *before* the stories began. What did the characters do, and what might have led to their circumstances?

❑ **34. Decide on a good cause, and figure out how to support it.** How can you help people who are less fortunate, or perhaps heighten awareness about issues relating to climate change, wellness, reading accessibility, or equal rights? You could also learn about preservation initiatives, and share information about causes such as protecting nesting turtles, safeguarding coral reefs, or saving endangered species like monarch butterflies, chimpanzees, tigers, whales, or sea lions. You might be able to raise money to advance your cause, for example, by making and selling bookmarks, or painting colorful planters for neighbors. Be a *unifier*—someone who brings people and causes together for the good of the broader community.

❑ **35. Try drawing a still life.** Perhaps a bowl of fruit? A vase of flowers? Have a look online at fruit bowls drawn by artists (for example, by Paul Cezanne), or flowers (for example by Vincent Van Gogh)—and check out the artists' use of color and light, and how they were able to convey a mood. Still life art became very popular several hundred years ago in Europe. Today, however, you can go online to see images of many past and present painters' creative renderings of different inanimate objects. What ordinary items (aside from fruit or flowers) can you paint and bring to life on paper or canvas?

❑ **36. Design a fancy hat—a "fascinator" or another kind of head covering.** Make it eccentric if you want. Wear it just for fun! Keep track of responses to your creativity. Host a tea party with an unusual theme, and invite everyone to wear a hat. Or learn to crochet and make warm, woolly hats for cold wintery days. Invite others to join you in making them, and then wear your creations while on nature walks or playing together outside.

❑ **37. Plan a virtual family vacation to a destination that's exotic or exciting.** Map out the trip. How will you get there? What should you take with you? Work out different activities you could potentially do there with your family. You can find travel brochures, maps, and blogs written by people who have gone before you. For example, you could plan a visit to Hobbiton, the fictional Hobbit village from the *Lord of the Rings* series in New Zealand. Or to Phillip Island in Australia to see the colony of Little Penguins, ideally at sunset when thousands upon thousands of these blue and white birds "parade" out of the water and waddle home to their nests. Or to places like Angor Wat, Machu Pichu, Masada, Ephesus, or Pompei to learn about different ancient civilizations. Make a travelogue or a creative journal.

❑ **38. Design some jewellery.** Use beads, embroidery thread, colourful stones, lanyard, or whatever else captures your interest. Create bracelets (for wrists, elbows, and ankles), necklaces (for around necks or stomachs), and rings (for fingers and toes). Make gift boxes and cards, and give the jewellery away as presents.

❑ **39. Devise a new and outlandish version of something ordinary or common place.** A light fixture, a table, a vase, a doorknob, a toilet paper holder, or a clock. (Have you ever seen the melting clocks in the 1931 painting *The Persistence of Memory* by Salvador Dali? Have a peek at that at The Museum of Modern Art online. https://www.moma.org/collection/works/79018 Awesome!) Basic and functional things don't necessarily have to be dull. For example, you might think that a garden patch is just standard and needs no modification. Well, I recently spotted a new design for a lovely raised and indented garden platform for people in wheelchairs who want to plant and tend their own flowers and vegetables. A clever, practical, and welcome creative idea turned real!

❑ **40. Become more aware of details.** Record your observations about something in the process of changing, such as a tree boasting different colors through the seasons, a sandcastle washing away, the progressing stages of a sunset, or the demise of a piece of fruit that's decaying and getting soft and wrinkly. What else can you think of that you can detail? (Consider: Why are details important for writers, artists, dancers, musicians, scientists, and other creators?) Practice *intentional noticing*, including attuning to differences, and perceiving similarities.

❑ **41. Stash your ideas.** Sometimes you'll have a great idea, or an *aha! moment* but you just can't do anything with it then and there. Don't discard it. Keep a stash of these gems in a box or a bowl (you can jot promising ideas on notepaper day or night), and go back to them when you feel the urge to be creative and have the time and inclination to extend your thoughts. For example, I just saw a microscopically detailed, grossly enlarged, and rather supernatural photo of a mosquito which reveals that this tiny creature has 100 eyes, 48 teeth, and 3 hearts. It finds its prey by using advanced heat sensitivity that can detect one thousandth of a degree Celsius.

It offers an anesthetic sting as it uses its 6 blades to bite, while using claws and hooks to hold on tight. Amazing! Eerie! (And rather unsettling.) It's the makings of a sci-fi story perhaps, but I just can't get my head around that now, so I've stashed the idea… What ideas can *you* keep hold of and possibly explore later?

❑ **42. Plan and enjoy creative adventures!** Here are some ideas: family camping, picnics, unbirthday festivities, games nights, scavenger hunts, geocaching, real or pretend campfires with s'mores, night sledding (in a well-lit spot), innovative triathalons, outings to a petting zoo or a farm, and holiday celebrations. These are all possibilities for fun! Take photos or find other ways to record the memories.

❑ **43. Meet Rufus.** He's a small toy teddy bear, and he's the beloved mascot in residence at Rufflets, a hotel in St. Andrews, Scotland. You can also find pictures of him online shared by families around the world who have adopted a Rufus of their own. There's a certificate, and specific instructions that accompany him. (He's to be given as much bed space as he wants, he must be cuddled a lot, and so on…) For example, Sari's Rufus gets daily exercise as she gently manipulates his arms and legs, and this routine is followed by hugs. My Rufus reclines against comfy pillows, and he has a window view. What care instructions would you provide to someone if you were going to ask them to look after your Rufus, another one of your favorite stuffed toys from early childhood, a beloved pet, or a cherished possession?

❑ **44. Learn to fold a towel or a napkin like a swan, or a dog, or an octopus, or a bird.** You can practice with paper (origami), and you can create your own unique representations, and teach others how to do the folding, too. (Cruise ships are noted for this perk. Passengers often find terry cloth "animals" awaiting them in their rooms.)

❑ **45. No two fingerprints are alike!** Use yours to create funny cartoon characters, or as parts of larger drawings that incorporate and reflect your distinctive imprint. By way of example, *pointillism* is a term that describes a style of painting that uses small dots of color that visually blend to form images. The technique was developed by artists George Seurat and Paul Signac. (You can learn more in art books, and have an online peek at one of Seurat's most famous paintings by googling *A Sunday on the Island of La Grande Jatte* [1884]). You can use fingerprints (or even toeprints or nose-tip prints) as your personalized dots! Also, have a look at Ed Emberley's *Great Thumbprint Drawing Book*, first published in 1977, and "reprinted" many times over.

❑ **46. Become more savvy about technological possibilities.** Emerging technologies continue to drive knowledge-gathering, communication, and research. Technology can also be a basis for creative production, and it can be woven into projects, learning experiences, and expression across different areas including writing, film, game design, mapping, and more. There are Artificial Intelligence companion feedback apps, and programs for enhancing drawings, animation, and story illustrations. However, be smart and maintain a healthy relationship with technology. Too much screen time can be problematic.

❑ **47. Let music move you.** All kinds of music! Opera; jazz; classical; country; marches; hymns; rhythm and blues; cultural favourites; early rock and roll; movie theme songs; disco; national anthems; rap; jingles... How does the music make you feel? Is it soothing? Invigorating? Does it tug at your heart or stir your imagination? Does it make you want to tap your feet or dance?

Watch young children as they respond to and interact with music. Better still, get involved by joining in, encouraging them, and sharing in their enjoyment as they become increasingly engaged with melodies and lyrics. For example, Canadian musician Nancy Kopman writes and sings songs that promote learning, confidence, and music appreciation for little ones. She says that *music connects hearts*, and that *singing with a child is an act of giving and receiving at the same time.* She delights groups of preschoolers *and* their parents, grandparents, siblings, and caregivers as she enthusiastically interacts with them by sharing songs, and introducing instruments and creative movement. She says, *music is comforting, reassuring, calming, exciting, nourishing, and nurturing at every stage of life.* https://nancykopman.com No matter what your age is, you can be an avid participant, and an encourager.

European composer Frederick Delius, said, *Music is an outburst of the soul.* Whether independently, or with others, you can benefit immensely from listening to and participating in various musical activities. This includes playing an instrument, composing, harmonizing, singing, moving to melodies, or listening quietly.

In an interview, modern-day composer, musician, and educator Hanne Deneire speaks to the creative power of music.

> *Music is the only art form that moves in so many different directions. A painting stays the same if you look at it five minutes later. Interpretation can grow but the work itself does not change. However, a piece of music develops over time and in space, and each performance is a new creation. Every musician will interpret the music in their own way. A composition develops creatively each time it is performed.*

How exciting is that? At her studio in Belgium, and by means of far-reaching technology, Hanne teaches children to compose music by providing instruction and encouraging their creativity. https://hannedeneire.info/welcome Bravo! Increase the music in *your* life!

❑ **48. Critique advertisements for fun!** Can you do a better job? Have a look at television, magazine, billboards, and other kinds of ads that are designed to entice people to buy things. Cars, food, furniture, toys, clothing… In what ways are the ads creative? How can *you* make them even more so?

❑ **49. Check out National Day calendars. What can you celebrate creatively?** Have a look at this website: https://nationaldaycalendar.com/calendar-at-a-glance/ As I write this, it's August 12th.

It so happens that today is International Youth Day! That's certainly something worth celebrating, and indeed there are creative youth-oriented events happening around the globe. It's also World Elephant Day (they're amazing animals); National Julienne Fries Day (my favorite kind); National Vinyl Record Day (I have lots of those stashed in my garage); and National Middle Child Day (siblings can creatively decorate and then share a cake). Tomorrow? It will be International Left-handers Day! Did you know that approximately 12% of the population are lefties? Singers Lady Gaga and Paul McCartney are lefties. Albert Einstein was a leftie, too. So were artists Leonardo DaVinci, and Michelangelo; composers Wolfgang Amadeus Mozart and Ludwig Van Beethoven; authors Lewis Carroll and Mark Twain; guitarist Jimi Hendrix; and scientist Marie Curie (who researched radioactivity and was the first woman to win a Nobel Prize). The creative outpourings of all these individuals have enriched the world—and that's also worth celebrating! Get creative like a leftie! Plus celebrate the current calendar day, whatever it is as you're reading this. (FYI—November 13th is officially World Kindness Day. But why wait till then to do something kind?)

❑ **50. Play with colors**. Get some paints and mix them in different ways. You don't have to actually *paint* anything with them right away. Just experiment with the combinations, mixtures of light and dark, unusual tones, and intensity (brightness or dullness of colors). Examine the full color spectrum. Make a chart or wheel showing what shades come from blending so if you want to, you can recreate the most interesting colors for use in art projects later.

❑ **51. Investigate other cultures**. Creative activities can vary from one culture to another, and you can enhance your own efforts and cultural awareness by learning about these activities. For example, Japan is known for a traditional style of painting (nihonga); haiku poetry (17 syllables, in three lines, 5/7/5), and beautiful gardens—tsukiyama (hill gardens), karesansui (dry gardens), and chaniwa (tea gardens). Two other examples of cultural treasure troves are Innuit art (including paintings, block printing, clothing, and carvings), and Amish quilts (which feature intricate stitching and beautiful patterns). Cultural influences from around the world can breathe new life into a creative project.

❑ **52. Combine creative modes**. Borrow ideas from one area of creative expression and use those to fortify or embellish another. For instance, still photographs or light enhanced technological images of dancers (ballet, jazz, waltz) can inspire new interpretive dance moves. Music can liven up a puppet show. An abstract mixed media artwork or collage can be designed using feathers, sports memorabilia, drawings, twine, magazine clippings, or myriad assorted materials. You might be able to elaborate upon a creative product by adding details to it or by filling in gaps in unexpected ways. Have fun!

❑ **53. Get a mentor**. Here's a very short descriptor of what's involved: *A mentorship is a supportive relationship between a learner and someone who is more experienced in a particular domain. (For example, sciences, creative arts, technology…). The mentor offers guidance, knowledge, and understanding.* A mentor can help you learn more about an area of interest. There are many advantages to mentorships, such as having fun; discovering resources; developing skill sets and practical applications; making new connections; experiencing intellectual challenge; and exploring critical and creative thinking opportunities. See my article on mentorships (at *The Creativity Post*) for further information, including how to structure a mentorship; additional benefits; considerations for kids, parents, and mentors; where to find a mentor; and more. https://www. creativitypost.com/education/mentorships_and_kids

❑ **54. Work on your ability to wait.** There's an old saying: *Patience is a virtue.* Creative expression, skill development, intellectual advancement—all these take time and patience. Advancement typically doesn't occur like a forceful wind-burst, or a flash flood. Have you ever planted a vegetable garden? Cast a fishing line? Scanned the night sky looking for a shooting star? These activities require you to wait. But there's the thrill of building expectancy! What will grow? What will bite? What will you see in the sky? And, how long will it take? Will it be frustrating? And what else should you do before something (if anything) happens? Author Luc de Clapiers wrote, *Patience is the art of hoping*. Hone your patience, and while you're at it keep hoping!

☐ **55. Revisit your previous creative ventures**. You may have some unfinished pictures you've drawn, or songs or stories you've written. They could be sitting around from when you were younger. Why not give them a fresh look and a makeover? How can you make them more interesting or exciting! Even a minor revision could be the start of something wonderful! I recently discovered a collection of stories that I wrote for a creative writing class I took about thirty years ago. The papers were in a file that I found when emptying out a cabinet. I'm looking forward to revisiting these stories, bringing them up to date, and figuring out possibilities for sharing them somehow.

☐ **56. What do you regret not trying—yet? Or what would you really like to try?** Make a list of experiences you'd like to have. (This is sometimes referred to as a *bucket list*.) You might want to do the following: go bungee jumping; swim with dolphins; be in a movie or television show; ride a camel; take a leadership course; fly in a hot air balloon; attend the Super Bowl (or the Masters Golf Tournament, the Wimbledon Tennis Championship, the NHL Stanley Cup Finals, or the Kentucky Derby); help rescue stray, lost, or abandoned animals; walk across a glacier; learn a new language; go on a safari; or…? What might help you become more fulfilled, or more informed, or perhaps more charitable? Of course, some desires, like wanting to become a firefighter, or pilot a helicopter, or win a marathon, may require extensive training and high levels of skill development. However, if you think resourcefully and creatively, and if you're motivated and able to invest the necessary effort over time, you may be able to work out the steps that might lead you toward checking off some of your bucket list aspirations—sooner as opposed to later.

❑ **57. Be a buddy**. Help a younger child be more creative in whatever area they choose. Encourage them and get involved in the pro-cess—the planning, the messiness, the fun. It may be game-playing, singing, cooking, or something else. Construct a birdfeeder; make slime; read or co-create a story and role-play it out loud; paint welcome stones and place them on the porch; or begin a scrapbook featuring the current season, or your favorite one. Do the activities together at a pace that's comfortable for your younger buddy.

❑ **58. Try another way of doing something, even though it may seem weird or scary**. This may be for better or for worse, but you can give it a shot. For example, my left knee was sore, especially when I would descend a flight of stairs, and my friend Mona told me to go down backwards—that it would take the pressure off my knee. I said, *No way, I'll fall.* (I didn't.) If you don't try something that may at first seem odd or somewhat risky, you'll never know if it works well. Be careful but be openminded. The bestselling book *Green Eggs and Ham* by Dr. Seuss (Theodor Geisel) consists of only 50 different words. Weird? Maybe. But the author accepted a challenge from his publisher, Bennett Cerf, and was determined to succeed. He often used visual flow charts while writing, and he was the first person to win a Pulitzer Prize for children's books. What can you do with just 50 different words? Or 100?

❑ **59. Create a book-lending centre**. It's like a little library—the books are free for the taking! You can design and build a small "house" or a showcase to feature the free books, and then place it on the lawn where anyone can take the reading material, or add their own. You can find out more here: https://littlefreelibrary. org/start/build-a-little-free-library/ This is a great way to share or exchange books *and* strengthen neighborhood connections.

❑ **60. Think of and use encouragements**. How can you encourage someone? You could offer complimentary words, a high-five, fist-pumps, a thumbs up, a pat on the back, hugs, or applause. Those are all great, but you could also create a set of "go-to" approaches—in your own style—to provide encouragement to others. Share these buddy-boosters with friends and family members, and agree to cheer each other on, and to support efforts and achievements.

Reflect… What's the nicest compliment you ever received? What made it special? How did you feel? What did you do next? What can you learn from this or carry forward?

The more that people encourage each another, the more they'll be inclined to stretch their boundaries and *choose* to be creative.

❏ **61. Go retro**. The word *retro* is short form for *retrospective*, from the Latin *retrogardi*, which means *move backward*. *Retro* refers to things from the past. Find out about antique boats and cars; vintage jewellery and clothing; or old-fashioned telephones, diners, or kitchen appliances. Talk to people (grandparents, seniors, friends, and neighbors) about their early memories, and check out popular early music genres, and old department store and mail-order catalogues. (Poke about online. Fascinating!) Go waaaaay back if you want to find out about what life was like in another era—perhaps the 1800s or early 1900s. What did people do? Eat? Wear? Keep track of what you learn about differences between today and yester-year. How can the design spirit of the past be tapped for your current and future creative projects? There's an (ahem) old expression, *What's old is new again*. Is it true, and if so *how*, and *why*?

❏ **62. Large vs small?** You can see the world's largest mailbox, the biggest chair, a massive birdcage, a giant pencil, a huge pair of wooden shoes, enormous windchimes, and more in Casey, Illinois. The town's people embraced a creative idea—to design these things so their little town would become a big attraction. It worked! By way of contrast, there are "miniature worlds," too. Doll houses are a prime example of this. You can use your imagination to make small-scale furniture, accessories, and anything else you choose to replicate in tiny form. (I visited Miniworld Rotterdam, and I was awed by the attention to the smallest detail. Literally! See https:// www.miniworldrotterdam.com/ENGindex.htm. And, there's also Little Canada, located in Hamilton, Ontario, and voted one of the province's top exhibits in 2022 https://little-canada.ca.) Creative ideas come in all sizes! Check out the *Guinness World Records* site for information on fascinating discoveries and achievements, big and tiny, across countless domains. https://www.guinnessworldrecords.com Get inspired!

❑ **63. Become more aware of descriptive possibilities**. Writers often have difficulty finding the right words to tell a story or convey a feeling. It's helpful to have a thesaurus to poke through options. (It could be a hard copy or an online platform—I use both.) However, it's also useful to spend time differentiating among common *and* atypical alternatives so you have a better sense of what might fortify your stories, poems, or song lyrics. Knowledge empowers! For example, here are several synonyms for *Joy: Happiness. Glee. Exuberance. Delight. Bliss. Pleasure. Gladness. Exhilaration. Rapture. Elation.* Lots of possibilities! Do they all really mean the same thing? What's the best word for revealing the essence of a particular moment, feeling, or set of circumstances? Increase and massage your vocabulary. *Knowing* and *choosing* the right words can raise the quality of your creative expression. Explore and understand synonyms for words or feelings that matter to you. Learning—and also playing with words—can be… a *joy*!

❑ **64. Know your own vibe.** Do you function best when it's quiet? When there's soft lighting? With or without immediate feedback? With ice cream or a bowl of homemade soup? At certain times of day or evening? With colored pencils, acrylic paint, or chalk? Know thyself. Respect your likes, dislikes, and inclinations.

❑ **65. Don't put things off.** Aim for *purposeful action* rather than procrastination. If you're tempted to avoid doing something creative (too difficult? time consuming? or maybe you're feeling lazy?) then think again. Procrastination is a way out, or a way of retreating or delaying but it is NOT a way forward. Be proactive! *Don't ever take 'can't' as the answer unless you've verified that it is against the law or against the power of physics.* Entrepreneurial 14-year-old Cole Summers—real name Kevin Cooper—wrote those words in his autobiography. You can read about his remarkable accomplishments in an article by Daryl Gibson, who describes this young boy's life and legacy. It's a riveting account, and it underscores the importance of making every moment-day-week-year-opportunity count.

❑ **66. Embrace messiness.** Cognitive psychologist Scott Barry Kaufman describes creativity as a messy business! Don't let sloppiness or clutter impede your creative energy. Be accepting of it. Create your own fun-filled, positive havoc. Here's my advice: *Romp freely through mud puddles, participate in musical jam sessions, try splatter painting, or do an improv performance. Doodle, dabble, splash, and experiment. Write with your other hand, brainstorm ideas, dance wildly, step outside your comfort zone. Get in touch with your creative side, and be open to letting messiness bring you happiness and creative fulfilment!* (Excerpted from "Mess for Success," Oct. 2022)

❑ **67. Repurpose odds and ends**. Inventor Thomas Edison, wrote, *To invent, you need a good imagination and a pile of junk.* Use your imagination and combine art, design, and "old stuff" to create "new stuff." There are apps and online sites to help you. For example, do you have loads of Legos lying around? If you lay them out on a table, take a picture, and upload it to *Brickit* (https://brickit. app), you'll receive a response with photos of creative things you can build. There's also an emoji mashup site you can explore. It's called *Emoji Supply Kitchen* (https://emoji.supply/kitchen), and it enables you to turn your overused or "ho-hum boring" emojis into creative new ones. (Thanks to author Jane Friedman, for these two app tips.)

You can take other about-to-be-tossed things and make the most of them, too. Why not create mosaic pictures from bits of broken plates or glass; sew doll quilts from scraps of fabric; use metal nuts, bolts, screws, and cutlery pieces to make a sculpture; or turn old puzzle pieces into picture frames or coasters? What stuff is lying around your home awaiting a renewed take? What have you got to lose? Consider these wise words from Friedman: *If we saw how much even the masters fail, we might feel reassured about our own abilities*. Use your abilities, ingenuity, and whatever materials you have lying around that you can repurpose, and don't hesitate to get creative!

❑ **68. Go outside more**. Let the marvels of nature stimulate your senses. Experience rain, sunshine, humidity, hail, and snow. Make an ice castle. Catch dandelion fluff and make a wish. Follow a squirrel, watch a butterfly, or record the melody of a robin, a cardinal, or a loon. Admire wildflowers, towering trees, and fields of wheat, corn, pumpkins, or cows. Appreciate the beauty of lakes, rock formations, cloud patterns, and waterfalls. Write, sketch, reflect, sing, or do a creative happy dance—on your own or with others.

❑ **69. Honor your feelings**. If you don't feel creative sometimes it's okay. In fact, that's to be expected. Who can be creative all the time? If you need a break, or you think you're being pushed too hard, or if you're "stuck," know that you're not alone in this. Take a breather. You'll be ready to be creative at some point when you feel the spark again.

❑ **70. Ask lots of questions.** Albert Einstein wrote, *Learn from yesterday, live for today, hope for tomorrow. The important thing is not to stop questioning.* Curiosity and inquiry are combustible—like rocket fuel—and can propel you to new heights. Teach yourself how to ask probing questions that invite thoughtful responses—not just questions that generate boring "yes" or "no" or "maybe" responses.

❑ **71. Look into mythology, legends, and folklore**. Discover fascinating tales about people from days-gone-by and from other-worldly lands, and characters who have special powers or who may seem mysterious, unbelievable, or heroic. Zeus, Poseidon, Apollo, and Aphrodite are just a few from Greek mythology. Also, comic book stories, illustrations, and movie characters can be fascinating—Wonder Woman, Superman, and Scooby Doo are examples. Graphic novels are full of intriguing individuals, too. You'll find them embroiled in complicated situations, and they may have unusual motives and inventive means of solving problems. Let creative stories and epic characters enliven your imagination.

❏ **72. Write a biography**. Who do you admire? Why? What's their story? Tell it in full! You could select an accomplished athlete, musician, family member, author, scientist, or entrepreneur—alive or deceased. What can you learn about their personal journey, including their creativity, resilience, and achievements? How could their experiences inform yours?

You might also think about writing your own story—that is, starting an autobiography—and you can keep adding to it over time.

❏ **73. Be flawsome**! It's okay to make mistakes—flaws don't mean you can't be awesome! For example, Post-it notes were accidentally created when Dr. Spencer Silver was looking into strong adhesives and discovered a glue that only stuck lightly, so it didn't bond heavily or damage things. The peelable stickies (which are great for brainstorming sessions), were launched in 1980. And do you know how chocolate chip cookies came about? In 1930, inn-keeper Ruth Graves Wakefield was making chocolate cookies, but she ran out of bakers' chocolate, so she chopped up chunks of chocolate instead. She thought they'd melt evenly through the batter. However, she ended up with chocolate chips, and a new delicacy was created! And, in 1950, when chef George Crum's customers complained that his potatoes were too mushy and thick, he decided to thinly slice and fry them—and potato chips were born. Three flawsome outcomes! Don't berate yourself if you create something flawed. It may be the impetus for something awesome!

❏ **74. Why? How?** Look into interesting facts and figures and see if the information you uncover might inspire you. For example, how do really high buildings and towers withstand storms? How do birds learn to fly? Why are temperatures rising, and how is that affecting polar bears or other animal species? What can you learn from research studies? One study indicated that the left side of the face is more photogenic than the right side. Is it true? (You can do a mirror check.) Another study, of skin cells, showed a new geometric shape called a scutoid that looks like a Y shaped prism with five surfaces on one branch and six on the other. What implications might this have for tissue construction and medical advances? The more you learn about science and the world, the more information you'll have to refer to, write about, draw, or use in other creative ways.

❑ **75. Cultivate inter-generational connections.** Get together and spend quality time with an elderly person you trust—perhaps a senior family member, a veteran, or a retired professional who worked in a field that's of particular interest to you. Listen to their stories, and perhaps record them somehow. What can their experience and successes over a span of a great many years teach you about resilience, creativity, and a strong work ethic? How did they overcome struggles? What advice do they have to share? (By the way, you can cultivate *international* connections, and *intercultural* ones as well.)

❑ **76. Mats matter.** There are place mats for tables, door mats for floors, rubber mats for showers, soft mats for babies to play on, and plastic car mats for (you guessed it) cars. There are mats located beside beds, and elsewhere in people's homes. Some mats are little, and some are big, but each mat presents an opportunity to be creative. Think of it as a "mat"erial canvas that you can decorate with patterns, drawings, or whatever you choose.

❑ **77. Motivate yourself.** There are MANY possible ways to get motivated, but I like the following 4-point motivational path— and it's easy for me to remember so I can repeat the R words to myself whenever I need a boost: *Rest. Revitalize. Reflect. Recommit.* However, you might prefer this one: *Play. Prioritize. Prepare. Persist.* Or *Connect. Communicate. Cooperate. Create.* Better still, get creative and devise your own personal motivational guide—or two!

I was a classroom teacher for a long time, and I always maintained a three-word motto that I strove to adhere to with my students: *Flexibility, Sensitivity,* and *Collaboration.* Each person in my classes also had their very own "guideposts." It was helpful to have these motivators, and to share them, too.

❑ **78. Self-advocate.** Be seen. Be heard. And be courteous! But be sure to convey your desire to exercise creativity at school. Be willing to help co-create opportunities to infuse creative expression into your assignments, activities, collaborations, and daily learning experiences. Chat with your teacher about how to facilitate this.

❑ **79. Value alone time.** Solitary interludes are opportunities to pay heed to your thoughts, recenter yourself amidst the busyness of life, and find calm. You can be productive without distractions, reinforce your independence, and focus on next steps for a task or for activating creative ideas. On page 105 of *Boosting Your Child's Natural Creativity*, authors Daniels and Peters say, *Periods of quiet, rest, and alone time are essential to creativity.* Solitude (like silence), *can* be extremely beneficial—but keep in mind that too much solitude can be disheartening, isolating, and lonely. Take care to balance your alone time with ample connectivity with others.

❑ **80. Just be lazy sometimes.** It's not sinful! Press the snooze button, swing in a hammock, or just float in a pool with friends. (Interestingly, *recreate*—to relax and enjoy, and *recreate*—to create anew—are the same word!) Take ownership of your right to laze about—occasionally. You can flip the action switch when you're ready. Meanwhile, let your laziness help you recharge if you need to strengthen your body or build up "the desire you require" to be more creative. Did you know that lazy-looking ducks floating serenely on the water are actually paddling beneath the surface? You, too, can float lazily but still be kicking around ideas...

❑ **81. Play with words.** Words are super-fun building blocks! They inform, catapult ideas, comfort, strengthen communication channels, provoke, and encourage. Words can be simple but powerful (like please and thanks); compound (like grasshopper); giggly (like sneezewort); tongue-tingling (like thorny thistles); unusual (like sassafras); or combined (like glisters, which is a blend of glistens and glitters—as in Shakespeare's *All that glisters is not gold*.) Words convey humor, attitudes, moods, and personality. There are antonyms, synonyms, homonyms, homophones, alliteration, and rhymes. Why not explore spoonerisms, oxymorons, hyperbole, malapropisms, idioms, onomatopoeia, and aphorisms? Investigate word games, recent dictionary additions, "retired" words, and word origins. Exchange ordinary words for compelling ones. (Ubiquitous. Fortuitous. Quanked. Zephyr.) Some topics, like technology, cooking, or sports, have specialized vocabulary that you could learn to use. For example, in skiing there are cat tracks (service trails); bunny slopes (beginners' hills); pizza and french fries (skis positioned in wedge or parallel formation); and big dumps (large snowfalls).

Explore the wonder of words! They can transform the way you think, speak, and act, and make expression more mellifluous! (For additional ideas, see "The Wonder of Words," at *The Creativity Post* https://www.firsttimeparentmagazine.com/the-wonder-of-words/)

❑ **82. Start off simply.** You can be playfully creative in your own backyard or neighborhood park. There's an old saying, *Less is more.* If you're a budding botanist, you can use a simple magnifying glass and a camera. If you aspire to be a structural engineer or an architect, mess around with pails and shovels and try reconfiguring sand, stones, or packing snow to construct something original. Down-to-earth, unfussy, tech-free, inexpensive activities can promote skill development, creativity, and joy.

❑ **83. Poke your memory.** Think back to things, places, and people who've peppered your past and that you remember fondly. Why not record the essence of these memories that made an impression on you? For example, your first time on a boat, horse, rollercoaster, or subway train; a story told to you by your grandparents about an adventure (or misadventure) they had; or a holiday experience that you particularly enjoyed. Write a story or a poem about it, make a scrapbook of photos relating to it, or create a short video clip. Think about how you can recapture those moments that matter, convey them creatively, and possibly share them with others.

❏ **84. Browse through books that focus specifically on aspects of creativity.** A library is a book-browser's paradise. You'll discover arts-and-crafts-oriented books, and "how-to" publications on almost anything you can imagine, such as photography, room decorating, interviewing, creative writing, game-making, robotics, calligraphy, nature-based explorations, and more. Plus, if you browse through "about creativity" books written primarily for parents, you'll find additional ideas. For example, there's loads of information that *you* can use in chapters 5 through 8 of *Boosting Your Child's Natural Creativity.* Topics include family gardens, doodling, drawing, painting, creative dramatics, local fieldtrips, and making movies.

❏ **85. Pick a letter of the alphabet! What can you create?** For instance, **M** is for **m**obiles, **m**iniatures, **m**arionettes, **m**urals, **m**irror art, **m**acramé, and **m**elodies. **P** is for **p**aper weaving, **p**eople watching, **p**otpourri, **p**udding **p**ainting, **p**eeping **p**eriscopes, **p**inwheels, and **p**uppets. Choose a letter, try an activity, and use your imagination!

❏ **86. Be a fan of fans**. People have used hand-held folding fans for centuries to keep cool, for ceremonial purposes, as elegant accessories, to whisk away pesky flies, and to improve air circulation. Fans can be made from paper, lace, wood, cardboard, plastic, or other materials. They can be created in different sizes, and they're often pleated, and beautifully painted. A fan can also be framed and hung on a wall as original artwork. The history of fans is long and fascinating (you can check it out!), and the various styles and cultural influences are wide-ranging. You can make a simple fan using paper—just fold and decorate. Or you can exercise further creativity and design one that's more elaborate. It's a fun activity, plus a fan comes in very handy in hot weather so it makes a fan-tastic gift.

❏ **87. Make an artistic assemblage of positive and negative space.** An *assemblage* is an arrangement or a putting together of parts. In art forms such as drawings and sculpture, the positive space consists of the figures (the shapes and forms), and the negative space is the emptiness that lies between them. Both positive and negative spaces are important. By paying attention to how you put these spaces together you can convey different feelings of lightness or heaviness, and create works of art with paper cut-outs, modeling clay, or other materials. You might want to consider signing up for a course in art, or art appreciation, or art history.

❏ **88. What about texture?** Works of art typically include a variety of lines, shapes, and colors. Those are three basic art elements. However, think of texture as well. Visual texture relates to what you can see, and tactile texture relates to what you can touch and feel. Objects can appear or be smooth, rough, bumpy, shiny, or matte (dull finish). And you can use different things like styrofoam, metal, ribbons, fabric, lace, wool, rope, felt, sparkles, wire, tissue paper, duct tape, and wood chips. Mixed-media forms of artistic expression—such as canvases, masks, collages, weaving, appliqués, and headpieces—become more interesting when you add unusual and contrasting design features. (A timeless resource for budding artists is the book *Art Connections, Level 6.*)

❏ **89. Explore balance and symmetry.** In dance, art, writing, and architectural structures, there is often *symmetry*. A butterfly's wings are symmetrical. The pattern is mirrored (the same) on both. There's balance in this. Personally, I like symmetry, although many people prefer things to be asymmetrical—that is, not the same, or even off-kilter. Look at art forms or photos and determine if what you see is arranged in balanced and symmetrical fashion, or appears to be positioned more informally. Have a peek at, and perhaps have fun with, the symmetry tool (and other features) in Procreate (https://procreate.com), an online design platform for Ipads, which is used by artists, animators, and illustrators. How might knowledge about balance and symmetry translate into your own creative endeavors?

❏ **90. What's your headline and lead story?** What if your life, or a part of it, was the focus of a major magazine or newspaper article? What would the piece be about? How would you convey the highlights? Write your own lead story. Illustrate it, too!

❑ **91. Don't fall into the trap of comparing yourself to others.** Be true to *you*. Other people may be more artistic, or technologically inclined, or coordinated. (Yup, all three as far as I'm concerned.) But why should comparisons stop you (or me) from putting forth creative energy in the arts, technology, or dance? Comparing accomplishments can be frustrating, undermine confidence, and foster resentment, especially if someone feels compelled to compete. It's not necessary. We all have different strengths in different areas. If you absolutely want to draw a comparison, think about how you can make today a more creative day than yesterday, or compare your younger creative self with your budding creative self as you go forward.

❑ **92. Ramp up your sense of humor.** Using humor can strengthen your creative expression. I'm not kidding! There are punny/funny signs that will make you smile and groan at the same time. A pun is a play on words, such as, *In search of fresh vegetable puns—lettuce know*. Or, *Tried to grab the fog—I mist*. There's, *If clowns attack, go for the juggler*. And, *My fear of moving stairs is escalating!* Plus, *I'm going to start collecting highlighters. Mark my words!* Finally, *Shredded cheese. The key to grate-ness.* The Indian Hills Community Center shares lots of pun-filled signs like these. https://www.facebook. com/IndianHillsCommunitySign/ Play with words, be funny, and create eye-popping original signs of your own! Or write jokes, stories, or verses that invite smiles, chuckles, guffaws, or belly laughs! Kidding around can be fun! Laughs are universal.

❑ **93. Challenge yourself!** Try something *finicky* such as mosaic pictures made with various kinds of seeds; *unusual* such as original sculptures made from pinecones, or wire hangers, or dried pasta; potentially (but not really) *creepy* such as gravestone rubbing; *technically demanding* such as robotics; or *difficult* such as intricate nail polish art. Take your time, take breaks as needed, and take pleasure in the creative process.

❏ **94. Take classes.** Register for a program or arrange for lessons to learn about a new area or a familiar area of creativity. Magic tricks? Cartoon drawing? Irish dance? Pottery? What piques your curiosity? What's being offered in your community? If learning experiences on something you're interested in are not available close by, where might you find them, or how might you initiate them close to home? You can ask others for suggestions or assistance.

❏ **95. Next level your thinking.** Take things up a notch and see where it leads. Whether you're expressing yourself in music, art, words, or whatever, take a shot at being more fulsome! For example, your culinary efforts can be tasty—or they could be mouth-wateringly delicious and creatively plated. And, if you're writing an interesting story, that's fine—but why not aim for a riveting story arc, cliff-hanger moments, dazzling descriptors, or fascinating characters? Try a full-blown creative upgrade in your next endeavor, whatever it might be!

Tennis sensation Serena Williams has embarked on business ventures (enterprising action off the courts). She has spoken about her learning curve, and the need to *raise her game* to be able to contribute to personal and collective successes. She's no stranger to hard work, and she knows the importance of self-motivation. You, too, can raise and then exceed your expectations!

❏ **96. Check and challenge your bias.** A *bias* is a particular way of thinking about or seeing things—in other words, your belief or point of view. For example, you may believe that spiders are scary, tunnels are uncomfortably confining, and everyone should be vegan. You're entitled to your opinion, *but* it might influence how you convey things about spiders, tunnels, or lamb stew. Similarly, when you read a book, look at a painting, or hear song lyrics, you're potentially being exposed to the creator's bias—which may or may not be evident. Be mindful. And, when you embark on an artistic project, pay attention to your own biases, and try to consider other viewpoints as well. For instance, if you're going to write a story about a skunk what's your bias? How can you broaden your perspective and possibly be more creative? (Are all skunks stinky? Must yours be black and white?) If you're painting a monster, what's your bias, and how might you alter or extend it? (Is every monster mean? Or large? Or toothy?) How might previous descriptions or viewpoints influence yours? You may share, reject, or wonder about other people's biases on a range of topics.

It's good to be *aware* of bias, and to give the matter some thought when you express yourself creatively. It's smart, too, to try and enlarge your point of view, especially if it tends to be narrow in some respects.

❑ **97. Borrow from other languages.** This is an inverted exclamation point: ¡ It's used in Spanish to indicate the start of an exclamatory statement. Likewise, there's this upside-down punctuation mark: ¿ It's used to denote the start of a question. Just an alternative way of communicating ideas! There are also TONS of interesting words that you can borrow from other languages to spice up your writing. For example, **Latin** (yes, Latin)—*ad nauseum* (extremely sick), *apricus* (extremely sunny), *umbra* (extremely shadowy), or *ad infinitum* (going beyond beyond, or extremely far); **French**—*avant-garde* or *de jour* (very cool), *bona fide* (very real), *jolie* (very pretty), and *blasé* (very boring); **Yiddish**—*chutzpadik* (being nervy, daring, brazen), *kvetch* (to complain), *shlep* (to drag), and *mensch* (an honorable individual); **Scottish**—dumfungled (exhausted); peelie-wally (pale or sickly); shoogle (shake); **German**—*kuddle-muddle* (an unusual mess), *morgenmuffel* (a morning grump), and *luftschloss* (an air castle or impossible dream). Foreign language possibilities are truly endless! Let them trigger your imagination—or luftschloss!

❑ **98. Digital games and learning experiences.** Online opportunities are an exciting frontline for creative exploration and expression—provided you're in a **safe** space. Many online gaming experiences (like Minecraft) have educational versions. There's always something new happening in areas of technology, gaming, and programmable toys, with updated styles, improvements, and add-ons.

Plus, you can create your own game world! For example, Nicholas developed a fantasy video game about odd insect forces and wild plant life inhabiting a planet filled with strange characters, exotic animals, hybrid vehicles, and elements of good and evil. He devised action-oriented scenarios and interesting conflicts. He also created a "sharing" package revealing selected illustrations, plotlines, and key aspects of his game design. What gaming or storyboard ideas do *you* have? You could create a computer-based game or a conventional boxed game. There are loads of gamers and researchers whose ideas might inspire you. Consider finding out more, including what motivated them, and what steps they took to bolster their creativity.

❑ **99. Something will happen...** What if you're in the middle of doing something creative, and you stall? Don't let it stop you! Just write *This spot saved for later.* Then jump ahead. It's not necessary to plug every gap in a story as you write, or include every detail of a poem, song, or picture. Move on and return to it another time. Think of it like a pothole in the road that you can fill in later.

❑ **100. Find like-minded people.** I saved this one for last. It's both sensible and uplifting to share your interests. It will extend your frontiers. So, be opportunistic! Scout for options. What clubs can you join or start? Reading? Chess? Improv? Debating? What community service initiatives exist (or should exist) in your area? What about teams—sports, competitive, mind games—that facilitate recreational or imaginative activities? Have you considered acquiring memberships at galleries? Museums? Theater venues? Or conservation areas? Involvement with other people who have similar interests has many advantages. For example, you'll develop new relationships, and you'll be increasingly motivated to use creative and other kinds of thinking skills. Most importantly, find people who are curious, brave, imaginative, and resourceful—and who will encourage you to ask questions, and to be increasingly open to creative possibilities.

Now it's up to you! Revisit and ponder. There are 100 points in the list above. Take time to review what "creativities" might have resonated for you, and how you've prioritized them, perhaps using the possible organizational options and tags suggested at the outset of this chapter. Then get started—one creative idea at a time!

Top Take-Aways from Chapter Eight

🔥 The suggestions here are starting points to help you kindle your creativity. There is no limit, however, to where you might find inspiration.

🔥 You can organize the 100 suggestions as you wish (there are some approaches to consider), follow up on those that are of interest, and add to the list if you want.

🔥 You can always go back to any part of this book for additional ideas and incentives to spark your creativity. Be sure to check out the resources and references at the end (coming up next), too.

Illuminating Resources and References:

You Can Be Creative!

(Also for Parents and Teachers)

In this section you'll find many sources of information. Much of the resource material that I cite within the previous eight chapters I've gleaned from people who have websites, who have written books and articles, and who give presentations as well. I accredit these people, and you can investigate their work if you're interested in finding out more about what they do, or if you want to learn more about certain things that I touch upon in these pages.

I also share here the names of individuals I quote throughout this book. They reflect a broad cross-section of people—from different countries, eras, and walks of life. If their words move you (as they did me), you can look them up and find out what else they've said or written that might inspire your thoughts or actions.

In addition, you'll find a mini glossary of some terms that I use, and that you might want to contemplate further.

Think about the many references that follow as representing embers. An ember is a glowing fragment that remains from a fire, and it can be fanned and revived—like memories, ideas, and emotions. There's so much more that you can explore, if you wish, by reflecting upon the knowledge you've acquired from reading, and then using the information below as embers, and your curiosity, resourcefulness, and effort as accelerants for creativity.

Books, Articles, and Other References Cited Within This Book

Babbitt, N. (2007). *Tuck Everlasting*. Square Fish Publishing.

Barkley, S. and Foster, J. (2022). "Co-creating a creative vibe: A 3-part series (for parents and kids) in conversation with Stephen Barkley." Podcast.

Baum, F. L. (1900). *The Wonderful Wizard of Oz*. George M. Hill Company.

Cameron, J. (Film Director) (2022). *Avatar: The Way of Water*. 20th Century Studio.

Carle, E. (1969). *The Very Hungry Caterpillar*. World Publishing.

Csikszentmihaly, M. (1997). *Creativity: Flow and the Psychology of Discovery and Invention*. Basic Books.

Daniels, S. and Peters, D. (2022). *Boosting Your Child's Natural Creativity*. Gifted Unlimited, LLC.

Delahooke, M. (2019). "The two life-changing qualities that make teachers extraordinary." Blog.

Delahooke, M. (2019). *Beyond Behaviors*. PESI Publishing.

Deneire, H. (2018). In "Appreciating music as a foundational aspect of creativity." *The Creativity Post*.

Dr. Seuss (Theodor Geisel). (1960). *Green Eggs and Ham*. Random House.

Emberley, E. (2005). *Ed Emberley's Great Thumbprint Drawing Book*. L. B. Kids Publishing.

Feldman, A. (2022). *When I Am Calm*. Gifted Unlimited, LLC.

Fleming, V. and Vidor, K. (Film Directors) (1939). *The Wizard of Oz*. (MGM Studios.

Foster, J. (2019). *ABCs of Raising Smarter Kids*. Gifted Unlimited, LLC.

Foster, J. (2017). *Bust Your BUTS: Tips for Teens Who Procrastinate*. Gifted Unlimited, LLC.

Foster, J. (2015). *Not Now, Maybe Later: Helping Children Overcome Procrastination*. Gifted Unlimited, LLC.

Frank, M. (1976). *I Can Make a Rainbow: Things to Create and Do… for Children and Their Grown-Up Friends*. Incentive Publications.

Friedman, J. (2022). *Electric Speed Newsletter*. Jane Friedman Media, LLC.

Gibson, D. (2022). "America's most remarkable kid died in Newcastle Utah—His legacy never will." *Deseret News*.

Gilman, P. (1988). *Jillian Jiggs*, Scholastic.

Gottesman, R. (2015). In "What drives children's creativity?" *The Creativity Post*.

Grant, A. (2021). "There's a name for the blah you're feeling: It's called languishing." *The New York Times*.

Harlow, T. (2022). *CIVIT Online Presentation*. (Cumbre Internacionale de Inteligencia y Talento).

Heitner, D. (2016). *Screenwise: Helping Kids Thrive and Survive in Their Digital World*. Routledge.

Hess, M. (2022). *I Used to Be Gifted*. Gifted Unlimited, LLC.

Hilbig, D. (2021). *The Adventures of Dillon Hilbig's Crismis*. Self-published.

Horn, M. B. (2022). "Agency and empowering individuals: An interview with Ian Rowe and Scott Barry Kaufman." *The Future of Education with Michael B. Horn*. Podcast.

Hurley, K. (2021). *The Stress-buster Workbook for Kids*. PESI Publishing.

Jackson, P. S. (2013). *Resilient, Calm, and Deeply Engaged, 27 Strategies*. Online presentation.

Kang, S. (2021). *The Tech Solution: Creating Healthy Habits for Kids Growing Up in a Digital World*. Penguin Canada.

Kaufmann, F. (2021). *Conversations with Colorado Association for the Gifted and Talented*. Online Presentation.

Kaufman, S. B. and Gregoire, C. (2016). *Wired to Create: Unravelling the Mysteries of the Creative Mind*. TarcherPerigee.

Kennedy-Moore, E. (2019). *Kid Confidence: Help Your Child Make Friends, Build Resilience, and Develop Real Self-Esteem*. New Harbinger Publications.

Kerr, B. (2016). *Take on Talents*, National Association for Gifted Children Video Clip.

Kinney, J. (2022). *Diary of a Wimpy Kid: Diper Overlode*. Amulet Books.

Lahey, J. (2016). *The Gift of Failure*. Harper.

Matthews, D. (2022). "Give the gift of gratitude this holiday season." *Psychology Today*.

Matthews, D. (2020). *Imperfect Parenting*. American Psychological Association.

Matthews, D. and Foster, J. (2021). *Being Smart about Gifted Learning*. 3rd Edition. Gifted Unlimited, LLC.

Milne, A. A. (1929). *The House at Pooh Corner*. Methuen and Company Ltd., UK.

Newman, S. (2014). *Little Things Long Remembered*. Iron Gate Press.

Orlando, J. (2021). *Life Mode On: How to Feel Less Stressed, More Present, and Back in Control When Using Technology*. Hardle Grant.

Pfeiffer, S. (2015). "Lessons learned from working with gifted and creative kids." *The Creativity Post*.

Prober, P. (2016). *Your Rainforest Mind*. GHF Press.

Ragan R.; Davis, W.; Farrell, T.; Hudak, J. R.; McCoy, G.; Morris, B.; Yoshida, N.; and Ellet, J. *Art Connections, Level 6*. (2005). SRA/McGraw-Hill.

Reynolds, P. (2012). *Sky Color*. Candlewick Press.

Reynolds, P. (2004). *Ish*. Candlewick Press.

Reynolds, P. (2003). *The Dot*. Candlewick Press.

Rowe, I. (2022). *Agency*. Templeton Press.

Rowling, J. K. (1997). *Harry Potter and the Philosopher's Stone*. Bloomsbury Publishing.

Silverstein, S. (2014). "Listen to the Mustnt's" in *Where the Sidewalk Ends*. HarperCollins.

Spielberg, S. (Film Director) (2022). *The Fabelmans*. Amblin Entertainment; Reliance Entertainment.

Tetreault, N. (2021). *Insight into a Bright Mind*. Gifted Unlimited, LLC.

Zakreski, M. (2021). In "Hope" at *The Creativity Post*.

Plus...

I've written extensively about creativity, so here are references to some additional material that's been published in the last while, and that I mention briefly within this book. These resources are accessible as noted below, and on the Resources Page at https://joannefoster.ca

"Mess for success" —*Best Version Media's Neighbours Magazines*, Oct. 2022.

"Early morning musings"—*The Creativity Post,* July 11, 2022.

Productivity Through Adversity. (Complimentary Resource Booklet). Gifted Unlimited, LLC. (2021).

"At ease—if they please." —*The Creativity Post.* June 8, 2021.

"The wonder of words!" —*First Time Parent Magazine.* April 4, 2021.

"Best learning environments." —*First Time Parents Magazine.* June 3, 2020.

"Help children embrace new beginnings." —*The Creativity Post,* Jan 4, 2020.

"Why community matters for children AND adults." —*GHF Dialogue,* 2020.

"Mentorships and kids." —*The Creativity Post,* Feb. 10, 2019.

"Aha! moments." —*The Creativity Post,* Dec. 2, 2018

Online Places and Platforms Worth Reiterating

I share some links in Chapter 8, and I also refer to several online places in other spots throughout the book. I've placed the URL (Uniform Resource Locator) information here as well for easy reference. Copy into your browser and explore!

About Kevin Cooper/ Cole Summers:
https://www.deseret.com/2022/8/22/23309244/cole-summers-died-newcastle-utah-warren-buffett-charlie-munger-bari-weiss-unschooled

Brainy Quotes: https://www.brainyquote.com

Brickit: (https://brickit.app

CNN News: https://www.cnn.com

Conversations with Colorado Gifted and Talented—
Featuring Guest Felice Kaufmann:
https://www.youtube.com/watch?v=-daCTrCHHIY

Emoji Supply Kitchen: https://emoji.supply/kitchen

Guinness World Records: https://www.guinnessworldrecords.com

Hanne Deneire: https://hannedeneire.info/welcome

Home Designed Little Libraries:
https://littlefreelibrary.org/start/build-a-little-free-library/

Indian Hills Community Center (pun-filled signs):
https://www.facebook.com/IndianHillsCommunitySign/

Little Canada: https://little-canada.ca.

Mini World Rotterdam:
https://www.miniworldrotterdam.com/ENGindex.htm

Museum of Modern Art:
   https://www.moma.org/collection/works/79018

Nancy Kopman: https://nancykopman.com

National Days Calendar:
   https://nationaldaycalendar.com/calendar-at-a-glance/

National Geographic for Kids: https://kids.nationalgeographic.com

Procreate: https://procreate.com

Rina Gottesman: http://www.rinagottesman.com

People Whose Words Are Quoted
Within This Book

Mini Glossary

Chapter One

Flow — the experience of being immersed in an activity

Ideation — the creation of ideas and concepts

Self-advocacy — speaking up for oneself

Chapter Two

Creatives — those who create (such as artists, authors, mimes, designers, and so on)

Divergent thinking — perceiving and looking at things in different or unusual ways

Idea traps — keeping ideas secure so you can release and develop them later

Mindfulness — the practice of focusing on the moment; paying attention to what's around you

Entrepreneurship — the business of making money from efforts, products, or services

Chapter Three

Transformative — having to do with change that affects how circumstances unfold

Ologies — forms of knowledge

Neuroplasticity — the brain's flexibility; the ability of networks in the brain to change, reorganize, and develop, and which enable learning and growth

Chapter Four

Screensmart being savvy about using digital devices, developing online connections, and navigating technology, apps, and platforms

Diversity differences in thoughts, actions, and ways of being

Heart strengths important personal attributes such as respect, compassion, humility, integrity, and forgiveness

Chapter Five

Wonderment the state of being in awe; appreciation, admiration, and astonishment

Rainforest a lush, thickly treed habitat and complex ecosystem

Calm curiosity pacing oneself, and experiencing life's marvels in manageable ways

Chapter Six

Juvenile a young eagle (up to five years old)

Chapter Seven

Languishing feeling blah or listless, and lacking initiative and effort

Self-actualization focusing on fulfilling your desires, and striving to become your best self

Proactical my own invented word to describe someone who is both proactive (takes initiative) and practical (is realistic and uses common sense)

Convenience	what's close by or readily available, and requires little effort or difficulty
Procrastination	putting things off or avoidance behavior

Chapter Eight

Tailwinds	providing momentum; empowering supports that give a boost to someone or something
Aha! moment	a time of recognition or realization, when an idea or inspiration suddenly comes to mind
Pointillism	a style of painting wherein small dots of color visually blend to form images
Bucket list	a wish list of experiences you'd like to have one day
Retro	referring to things from the past
Flawsome	a melding of flaw and awesome, suggesting that it's fine to embrace flaws, and recognizing that they can co-exist with awesomeness
Assemblage	an arrangement, or the putting together of parts
Symmetry	a mirrored pattern; the same or equal on both sides
Bias	a particular way of thinking about or seeing things; your belief or viewpoint

About the Author, Joanne Foster, Ed.D.

How do you know if the author of a book about creativity is actually creative?

You may not—unless they tell you!

So, here's what I think you might want to know about me. Read on if you're curious.

I'm a parent, grandparent, teacher, and educational consultant. (Ed.D. is short form for Doctor of Education. I don't have medical credentials, but I do have certifications and a lot of experience when it comes to learning—and learning about learning, and creativity.) I've taught extensively in public and private schools, and in university settings, and I've been on education advisory boards, too.

This is my eighth published book. I've loved writing ever since I was a little girl. I especially like bringing creative ideas to life. Each book (or article or presentation) that I've written started from a spark; that is, a thought or series of thoughts, that became a scorching hot idea. Then that idea evolved into words, paragraphs, and sometimes chapters. And each experience of writing has made me more fulfilled. Writing—like music, laughter, love, nature, and kindness—helps to nourish my soul.

I've found that authorship is intense, purposeful, challenging, and gratifying. It's an activity that offers a creative outlet, and opportunities for unbounded self-expression. My writing experiences have been transformative in that they've given me different perspectives into who I am, what I want to convey, what's central to my being, and how imaginative I can become. Even when I focus on "serious" topics, my writing represents a creative outpouring because of how I choose to communicate ideas. I write mostly about creativity, intelligence, procrastination, and children's well-being because these topics are meaningful to me and, hopefully, are relevant for others, too. I invite people of all ages into my literary playground.

Whenever I write, I have the freedom to assemble concepts creatively, and the option to reveal my reflections. This increases my self-awareness. It also leaves me vulnerable and takes guts, but I do it anyways because creative expression matters so much to me. Even though I lay bare my opinions, knowledge, values, and ways of thinking, it's worth going out on that limb. As my writing and creativity unfold, I embrace my *everlasting vision of the ever-changing view* (Carole King, 1971).

I realize I must continue to catapult my creative energy, capture my ideas (and ideals), and recognize the wonderment of that which is around me—what I've experienced, and what I'll encounter in the years ahead. I must choose to be creative, to invest in my personal and professional growth, and to nurture fresh extensions of myself. It's an active process, and as the world changes, I'll have to adapt, think creatively, and remain open to recreating notions and outcomes—and to sharing them as well. I may leap back and forth between innovative, scholarly, and pedestrian thinking, but as I traverse roads and bridges, I appreciate the joy of self-actualization and creative thought, and I'm grateful. I draw from personal experience, but also from the rich insights, research, energy, encouragement, and imagination of others.

If, over time, your creative quests and mine should follow similar paths, that would be lovely. If we should diverge, that might be even better. The more far-reaching and extensive the search for and understandings of what matters, the closer the stars.

Let's explore! Let's create!

Reflectively,

Joanne Foster, Ed.D. – https://joannefoster.ca

Other Books by the Author:

Being Smart about Gifted Learning: Empowering Parents and Kids Through Challenge and Change, 3rd Edition (Co-authored with Dona Matthews)

ABCs of Raising Smarter Kids: Hundreds of Ways to Inspire Your Child (Illustrated by Christine Thammavongsa)

Bust Your BUTS: Tips for Teens Who Procrastinate

Not Now Maybe Later: Helping Children Overcome Procrastination

Beyond Intelligence: Secrets for Raising Happily Productive Kids (Co-authored with Dona Matthews)